GREECE

AN ARCHAEOLOGICAL GUIDE

Wojciech Machowski

Translated by Ian Jenkins

Cover and interior design by Karolina Kawecka

First Edition

ISBN: 978-83-935757-1-8

www.archaeoguides.com

CONTENTS

INTRODUCTION

As early as the times of the *Imperium Romanum*, it was already a popular activity to travel around Hellas, visiting the most important cities, sanctuaries and cult places along the way. By doing this, it was possible to discover the history, mythology and beliefs of the Greek civilisation, which were so admired by the ancient Romans. One such traveller was Pausanias. His description of his travels, which has been preserved to our times, was my personal guide to Ancient Greece.

Pausanias embarked on his journey nearly 2000 years ago. Although it sounds improbable, through holding a translation of his work in our hands today (at sites such as the Acropolis of Athens, the agora of Corinth or the sanctuaries of Olympia and Delphi), one can envisage the remains of the wonderful buildings he once admired from his perspective. It is almost like going back 2000 years in time. In certain cases, such as at Mycenae, thanks to the work of several generations of archaeologists, it is possible to see a great deal more than Pausanias was able to. In others, such as at Sparta, the opposite is true. In these cases, only thanks to Pausanias' description is it possible to imagine how they would have looked in ancient times. Today, the modern buildings of these cities largely cover the former roads, squares, buildings and monuments.

Pausanias was born around 115 CE, probably in the area of Magnesia ad Sipylum (modern day Manisa), which lies in the western part of Asia Minor. It is believed he died around 180 CE. Pausanias today would have been termed a traveller, geographer and art historian. During his lifetime, he visited many sites, including Antioch in Syria and Jerusalem in Judea. He also saw the pyramids of Egypt, the Macedonia from which Alexander the Great had emerged and the then capital of the world, Rome. However, his most famous journey was his visit to Greece and in particular to the part which at the time belonged to the Roman province of Achaea.

The main fruit of this final trip was the guidebook, "Description of Greece" (in Greek, '*Periegesis tes Hellados*'), which was written between 160 and 180 CE. In this work, Pausanias described the lands of Greece which he visited, beginning with Attica, where he mainly focused on Athens. He then made his way to the Peloponnese, where he journeyed to Corinth, Argolis (seeing the cities of Mycenae and Epidaurus with its famous Sanctuary of Asclepius), Laconia (Sparta) and Messenia.

The next two chapters of his guide were dedicated to descriptions of Elis with its famous Sanctuary of Zeus at Olympia. The two final chapters of his work were dedicated to central Greece, where he journeyed to Boeotia,

as well as the smaller Phocis with its marvellous Sanctuary of Apollo at Delphi.

In more recent times, Pausanias' guide has become an invaluable source of information for many generations of archaeologists, historians and geographers. Whilst wandering through the cities of Greece in the 2nd century CE, Pausanias not only listed the finest monuments, but also often gave an exact description of their location. The true value of his work can easily be appreciated through reading the excavation reports of archaeologists at work in Greece or through a perusal of the works of modern historians of ancient times, who have found information in his work confirming the most important events of the ancient world. Researchers specialising in religious history can also find a vast array of information in his descriptions about local customs, myths and cults. Apart from monuments and legends, Pausanias also described the fantastically beautiful landscape of contemporary Hellas with its mountains, rivers and springs. Some of the information must, however, be approached with caution. Like every human being, Pausanias also made errors. The most common problem in his work is that mythical and historic events are often not differentiated. On the other hand, it must be remembered that the ancient Greeks believed the myths to be a part of their history and so Pausanias, who modelled his work on theirs, was not alone in the practice of blurring reality with myth.

During his journey across Hellas, Pausanias visited tens of smaller and larger cities, villages and sites which were connected to local cults and historical events. I have decided to present only the ones I consider most important. In my selection process, it was often not only the significance of the cities (e.g. Athens, Olympia, Delphi), but also their unique locations (e.g. the Menelaion, Sounion), the state of preservation of their monuments (e.g. Mycenae) and their importance in the events of Greek history (e.g. Corinth, Sparta) which prompted their inclusion. I am deeply convinced that all of these places are not only worthy of a place in this series, but are also worth visiting as you follow Pausanias on your own journey across Hellas.

The Parthenon. South-east corner of the temple.

Lying in Attica, on the Saronic Gulf, Athens was the most important centre of Greek art and civilisation. The mythical founder of Athens and its first king was Cecrops, from whom the original name of the city, Cecropia, derived. The present name comes from Athena, who became the patroness and protector of the city following a vote by representatives of its oldest families.

The rock elevation of the Acropolis lies in the heart of Athens and was the religious centre of the city from around the 8th century BCE. To the north of the Acropolis is the Agora, formerly the political, economic and community centre of Athens. The 'Roman Agora' was also located here, a trade centre erected in the period of Roman domination. Three hills lie to the west of the Acropolis (the Areopagus, the Pnyx and the Hill of the Nymphs), which were all important gathering areas for Athenian citizens.

To the south-east of the Acropolis, in the valley of the Ilisos river, lie the remains of the imposing Temple of Olympian Zeus, as well as the now totally reconstructed Panathenaic Stadium, with a capacity of 50,000.

Athens was once divided into six districts: Diomea, Kerameikos, Cydathenaion, Kollytos, Limnai and Melite. During the rule of Emperor Hadrian, another district, known as the City of Hadrian or Hadrianopolis, was created. Athens also possessed two trading ports (the famous Piraeus and Phalerum) and one military port (Mounichion).

Introduction

Athens is the place where most tourists choose to begin their adventure across ancient Greece. Although it is admittedly the most important point of any such journey, it should not be apportioned too much time.

The capital of Greece is a huge, modern city with all of the advantages and disadvantages that this entails. Unclean air, transport problems and inflated prices can all be found here.

For this reason, it is not worth spending more than two or three days in the capital, a period which should be perfectly sufficient to fit in all of the ancient remains.

For those who would like to sightsee following a relatively intensive schedule, the itinerary laid out below can be adopted:

Day 1: The Acropolis – The Athenian Agora – Kerameikos – The National Archaeological Museum.

Day 2: Hadrian's Library – The Roman Agora – The Olympieion – The Southern Slope of the Acropolis – The Acropolis Museum.

Today, the remains of ancient Athens are scattered across various areas of the modern city. They can be visited following the itinerary suggested here or in a completely different order of your own choosing.

DAY 1:

The Acropolis

The Acropolis is an absolute must-see for lovers of antiquity. Even with very little time on your hands, this rock elevation, once the religious heart of Athens, must remain your top priority. When planning a visit to the Acropolis, however, it must be remembered that it will most likely be swarming with group tours. If you wish to admire this wonderful monument in a somewhat more intimate environment, it is therefore necessary to arrive in the early morning or late afternoon. A visit to the Athenian Acropolis should not take any longer than around two hours. Afterwards, it is possible to continue to the Acropolis Museum located below its southern slope (although this is left to the second day in our suggested itinerary).

There is but one entry to the Acropolis. It affords no other, being precipitous throughout and having a strong wall. (Pausanias: 1.22.4)

The Athenian Acropolis. View from the Hill of the Muses.

The Athenian Acropolis. View from the Areopagus.

The Athenian Acropolis is positioned in the centre of the city on a rock elevation (around 157 metres above sea level) which has been inhabited continuously since Neolithic times (5th millenium BCE).

During the times of the Mycenaean civilisation (13th century BCE), the hill became the headquarters of the local leader. A mighty citadel surrounded by a cyclopic wall was therefore built, within which the palace of the ruler must have stood. Below was an underground spring, down to which a rock-cut path led.

In the 8th century BCE, the Acropolis became the religious centre of the rapidly developing city. Buildings from Archaic times (such as the Old Temple of Athena) were, however, utterly destroyed during the Persian invasion of 480 BCE. Reconstruction of the Acropolis only began after the signing of a peace treaty with the Persians ('The Peace of Callias') in 449/448 BCE, with Pericles the main driving force behind it. This work was overseen by the already famous Phidias, whose co-architects included Ictinus, Callicrates and Mnesikles.

Amongst the numerous cult buildings to be found on the Athenian Acropolis, three have stood the test of time fairly well: the Parthenon (built from 447 to 438 BCE), the Erechtheion (421 to 406 BCE) and the small, Ionic Temple of Athena Nike (425 to 424 BCE). The monumental entrance (propylaea), which was built between 438 and 432 BCE, is another example of

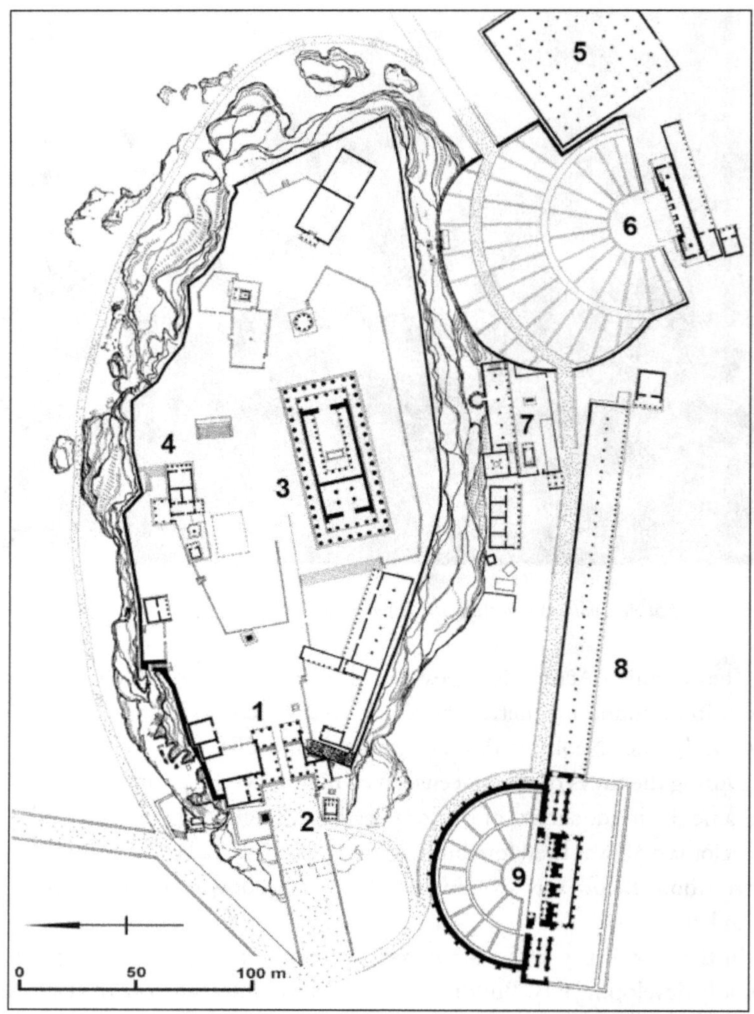

Plan of the Athenian Acropolis and its Southern Slope: 1 – Propylaea, 2 – Temple of Athena Nike, 3 – Parthenon, 4 – Erechtheion, 5 – Odeon of Pericles, 6 – Theatre of Dionysus, 7 – Temple of Asclepius, 8 – Stoa of Eumenes II, 9 – Odeon of Herodes Atticus (after Travlos 1971, fig. 91).

a building to have survived here. Other cult buildings of which only the level of the foundations have survived are: the Old Temple of Athena, the Sanctuary of Zeus Polieus ('Guardian of the City'), the Sanctuary of Athena Ergane ('Patroness of Craftsmen and Artisans'), the Sanctuary of Artemis Brauronia and the Temple of Augustus and Rome. The marvellous walls running around the hill, the remains of the Chalkotheke, the House of the

Arrephoros and small sections of fortifications from Mycenaean times can also be admired here.

The gateway has a roof of white marble, and down to the present day it is unrivalled for the beauty and size of its stones. (Pausanias: 1.22.4)

The Acropolis is entered today, as it was in the past, through a monumental entrance gate or 'propylaea'. Its construction began in 438 BCE and it was designed by the architect, Mnesikles. However, work was halted in 432 BCE and was never completed. This Doric construction consisted of a central building lying on an east to west axis, which performed the function of a gate, and two side wings (north and south). Both façades on the eastern and western sides contained six Doric columns, whilst two rows of three Ionic columns divided the central corridor into three passages. The middle one possessed a ramp which animals destined to be sacrificed were led up, whereas the side ones were intended for humans. The metopes and gables of the propylaea were bereft of any kind of sculptural decoration, whilst the side wings, which were fronted by porticos, were built on high rock platforms. The walls of a small room situated within the north wing (the 'Pinacotheca') were, however, decorated with pictures by famous Greek painters such as Polygnotus and Aglaophon. Pausanias mentioned the paintings which survived to his times, which included a depiction of Diomedes snatching a wooden statue (*xoanon*) of Athena from Troy and Perseus' return with the head of Medusa.

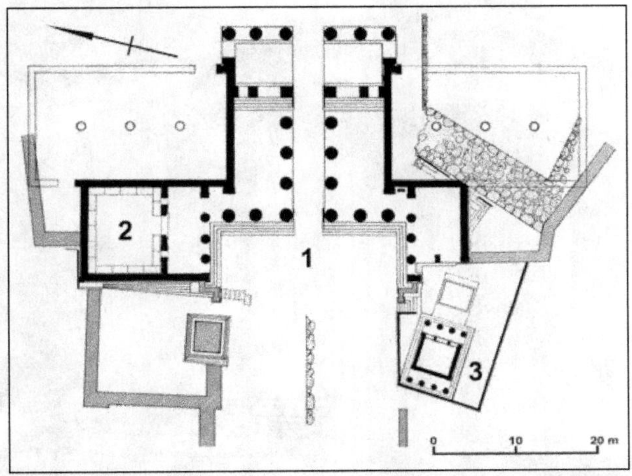

Plan of the Propylaea and the Temple of Athena Nike: 1 – Propylaea, 2 – Pinacotheca, 3 – Temple of Athena Nike (after Travlos 1971, fig. 614).

On the right of the gateway is a temple of Wingless Victory. (Pausanias: 1.22.4)

Just in front of the Propylaea itself, an imposing stone bastion can be seen to the right, upon which is the Temple of Athena Nike. This small building was constructed between 425 and 424 BCE following a design by Callicrates. It is an Ionic tetrastyle amphiprostyle building (four columns in its façade and also to the rear) with measurements of 5.44 by 8.27 metres and is made entirely of Pentelic marble. A continuous Ionic frieze running around the whole building was located above the architrave of the temple. It presented a gathering of the gods, who were watching fights (on the eastern part), as well as battle scenes. These were of the Persian wars (on the western part), the Battle of Plataea (the southern) and of Greeks fighting on horseback (the northern).

The platform on which the temple stood was surrounded by a marble balustrade. It was decorated by bas-reliefs presenting the celebrations following the Athenian victory over the Spartans, as well as the offering of sacrifices. The most famous bas-relief of the Temple of Athena Nike was that of 'Nike Adjusting Her Sandal', probably the work of Callimachus. It is currently housed in the Acropolis Museum.

As you enter the temple that they name the Parthenon, all the sculptures you see on what is called the pediment refer to the birth of Athena, those on the rear pedi-

The Temple of Athena Nike.

The Parthenon. West Façade.

ment represent the contest for the land between Athena and Poseidon. The statue itself is made of ivory and gold. (Pausanias: 1.24.5)

After passing through the Propylaea and entering the sanctuary, we see the monumental Parthenon (the largest temple of the Acropolis), which is dedicated to the goddess, Athena. Numerous statues stood on the way to it, amongst which Pausanias mentioned a marvellous one of Athena Promachos ('leading into battle') chiselled by Phidias. The glare emanating from the blade of the spear which the goddess held was supposed to be so bright that it could even be seen by ships sailing near Cape Sounion.

Work on the building of the Parthenon began in 447 BCE and lasted until the consecration ceremony of the temple in 438 BCE, when the colossal statue of Athena Parthenos ('the Virgin') was put into place. However, work continued on its sculptural decoration until 432 BCE. Two magnificent architects, Ictinus and Callicrates, are believed to have created the Parthenon together.

The temple was made entirely of Pentelic marble. It was a Doric peripteros measuring 30.86 by 69.51 metres with eight columns in its façades and seventeen on its longer sides. The central part of the temple consisted of a cella (fronted by a small pronaos), which contained the previously mentioned chryselephantine Statue of Athena by Phidias. The cella was divided into a nave and two aisles and contained a colonnade on two floors which ran around three sides of the room. To the rear was a square opisthodomos, within which stood four Ionic columns.

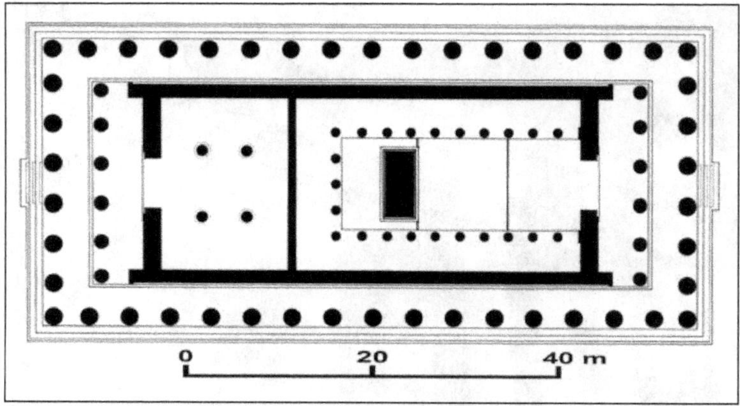

Plan of the Parthenon (after Travlos 1971, fig. 564).

The sculptural decoration of the Parthenon was an unusual mix of gables decorated with sculptural collections, a Doric frieze which ran around the exterior of the building and a continuous Ionic frieze on the arcades of the cella walls. The metopes depicted the Gigantomachy (to the east), the Amazonomachy (west), the Centauromachy (south) and scenes from the Trojan War (north). On the Ionic frieze (nearly 160 metres in length) was a depic-

The Erechtheion. View from the South-West.

tion of the Panathenaic Procession with the gods watching from the Acropolis, whilst the decoration of the gables displayed the mythical birth of Athena (on the east side) and the dispute between Athena and Poseidon over the rule of the city and the whole of Attica (on the west).

There is also a building called the Erechtheum. Before the entrance is an altar of Zeus the Most High, … Inside the entrance are altars, one to Poseidon, on which in obedience to an oracle they sacrifice also to Erechtheus, the second to the hero Butes, and the third to Hephaestus. (Pausanias: 1.26.5)

The Erechtheion is located in the northern part of the Acropolis. This construction was built (with interruptions) between 421 and 406 BCE, most probably following a design of Mnesikles or Philocles. It is an Ionic temple made of Pentelic marble, which was partly taken from the site of the Old Temple of Athena after the Persians had destroyed it.

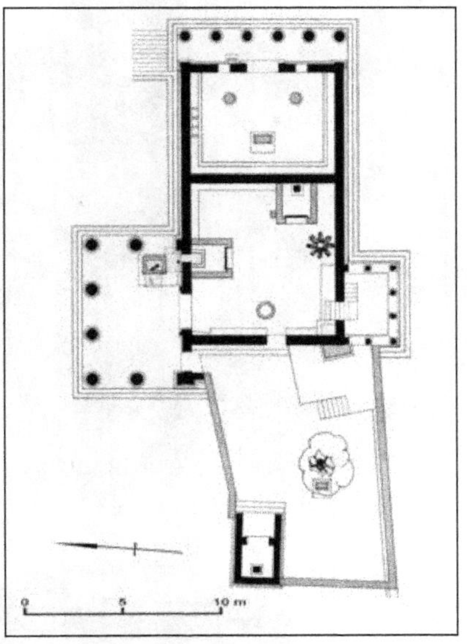

Plan of the Erechtheion (after Travlos 1971, fig. 281).

It was an unusually shaped building and contained cult places of several gods within it: Athena, Poseidon, Zeus Hypatos ('the most high'), Hephaestus and the Athenian heroes, Erechtheus and Butes. The grave of the legendary founder of Athens, Cecrops, is supposed to have been found here, as well as the rock which Poseidon is said to have struck during his dispute with Athena over the rule of Athens and Attica and the sacred olive tree then offered to the Athenians by Athena herself.

The multi-levelled façade of the Erechtheion was hugely varied. A façade in Ionic hexastyle form faced east and from here the cella could be entered through a small pronaos. The cella probably contained altars of Poseidon, Erechtheus, Hephaestus, Butes and Zeus Hypatos (just before the entrance). The northern side contained a six-columned Ionic portico fronting the entrance to the main hall of the Erechtheion, which was dedicated to Athena. The famous wooden statue (*xoanon*) of Athena Polias ('Protector of the City') was located here, as well as the grave of Erechtheus and the sacred snake.

The Erechtheion. Northern portico.

The western façade had a small, adjoining courtyard containing the sacred olive tree of Athena and the tomb of Cecrops. The southern façade, meanwhile, was decorated with the architectonic decoration for which the building is best known, the Caryatid Portico. This portico consists of six female figures, who act as columns. The adornment of the Erechtheion was completed by a continuous Ionic frieze situated above the architrave, which would have shown scenes depicting the life and deeds of Erechthonius.

The Athenian Agora

The Athenian Agora is the former political and economic heart of the city and another must-see for those fascinated by antiquity. This is due not only to the nearly

The Erechtheion. The Caryatid Portico.

The Athenian Agora. View from the South.

entirely preserved Temple of Hephaestus (a rarity in modern day Greece), but also because of the Portico of Attalos II, which has been wonderfully reconstructed by American archaeologists. The latter construction now houses the Agora Museum, which presents objects discovered over nearly 100 years of archaeological excavation. They are in chronological order and it is thus better to begin a visit to the museum from its southern side (located closest to the Acropolis). The whole visit to the Agora (including the museum), depending on your pace, physical condition and interest in individual monuments, should take between two and three hours.

The Athenian Agora was already inhabited in the Late Neolithic period (4,000–3,000 BCE) and a necropolis was located here in Mycenaean times.

In the Early Iron Age, apart from the still functioning necropolis, living quarters also started to appear, a fact which is attested by the discovery of the remains of household pits by archaeologists. The Agora began to play a civic role in the 6th century BCE, when buildings intended for public use began to be constructed. These included altars and buildings for government officials.

After the Persian invasion destroyed the Agora, reconstruction and development work was undertaken. During this time, complexes such as the Stoa Poikile (475–450 BCE), the Old Bouleuterion (around 470 BCE), the monumental Tholos (containing a dining hall for officials) (470–460 BCE), the Temples of Hephaestus and Athena (449–415 BCE), the Stoa of

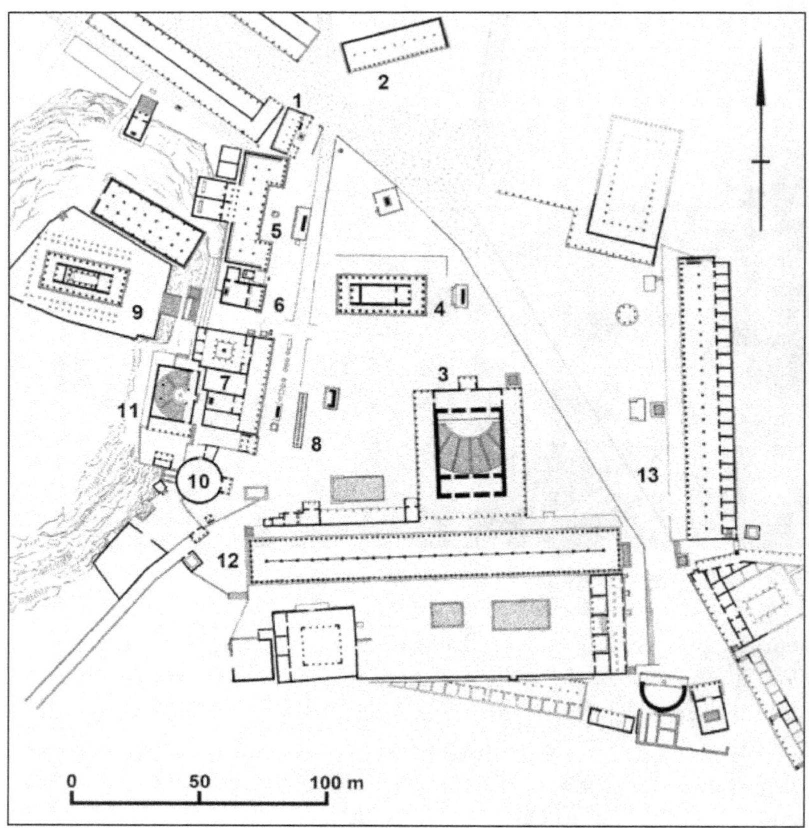

Plan of the Athenian Agora: 1 – Royal Stoa (Portico), 2 – Stoa Poikile, 3 – Odeon of Agrippa, 4 – Temple of Ares, 5 – Stoa of Zeus, 6 – Temple of Apollo, 7 – Metroon, 8 – Monument of the Eponymous Heroes, 9 – Temple of Hephaestus, 10 – Tholos, 11 – Bouleuterion, 12 – Central Portico, 13 – Stoa of Attalos II (after Thompson, Wycherley 1972, pl. 8).

Zeus Eleutherios (the Liberator) (430–420 BCE), the South Stoa (430–420 BCE) and the New Bouleuterion (the end of the 5th century BCE) were all erected. In the Hellenistic period, further edifices were constructed, including the Central Stoa (around 180 BCE) and the Stoa of Attalos II (around 150 BCE).

In Roman times, the majority of building work on the Agora was focused on the renovation and development of existing buildings. New constructions included the Odeon of Agrippa (around 15 BCE) and the relocation of a temple from outside Athens, which was then dedicated to Ares (also around 15 BCE).

Archaeological excavation of the Athenian Agora began in 1859. It was initially conducted by members of the Greek Archaeological Society before it was taken over by Americans in 1931.

Pausanias entered the Athenian Agora from the north, just as the majority of tourists do today. Before entering the site itself, however, we should focus our attention on the parts of the Agora (uncovered by American archaeologists) which extend along Adrianou Street.

First on the right is what is called the Royal Portico, … (Pausanias: 1.3.1)

In the north-west corner of the Athenian Agora, just next to a section of the former Panathenaic Way (currently between the bustling, tourist focused Adrianou Street and the tracks of the metro), are the remains of the Royal Portico (*stoa basileios*), one of the first and most important public buildings of Athens. It was used as the seat of the royal archon (*archon basileus*), who was the highest ranking official of Athens. He was responsible for religious matters and legislation and was helped in his work by two assistants. A marble tablet presenting a full list of the laws of Athens was displayed here.

The building itself was relatively small and modest for a portico as it was merely 7.57 metres wide and 17.72 metres long. Its front possessed eight Doric columns, within which four supports (initially only two) were positioned. Its rear section contained long stone benches and designated thrones for the most important personages. The erection of the portico dates to the end of the 6th century BCE, but it was later totally rebuilt, most probably after its destruction by the Persians. The two protruding side wings were added at the turn of the 5th and 4th centuries BCE. They contained new copies of the legal code of the city displayed to public view. A stone base was discovered between the side wings on the axis of the building during archaeological investigation. It dates to the 4th or 3rd century BCE and would once have held a statue of one of the Greek goddesses or a personification (e.g. of good fortune). The later fate of the portico is unclear, although it was probably destroyed or damaged by invading Heruli in 267 CE and then rebuilt. The identification of the building as a royal portico is, however, certain. This is thanks to both Pausanias' description and two inscribed bases of hermae discovered *in situ* on the steps of the building, which were dedicated by the royal archons.

As you go to the portico which they call painted, because of its pictures, there is a bronze statue of Hermes of the Market-place, and near it a gate. (Pausanias: 1.15.1)

During the course of recently conducted excavations to the north of the Agora between the current Adrianou and Astiggos streets, the discovery of the remains of a portico described by Pausanias as the Stoa Poikile ('Painted Stoa') caused a sensation. This portico was constructed in the Doric style, although its interior possessed Ionic columns. It was mainly made of limestone, but also contained sandstone and marble (for example on the capitals of the interior columns). Pottery found during research of the site suggests that the building dates to around 470–460 BCE.

The Stoa Poikile was one of the best known buildings in ancient Athens and its name and fame were made by the series of pictures which adorned it. These were created halfway through the 5th century BCE by the greatest painters of ancient Greece, such as Polygnotos of Thasos, Micon and Panaenus. Six centuries later, around 150 CE, Pausanias was still able to describe four of these: The Battle of Oenoe (between the Athenians and the Spartans), the Amazonomachy, the Taking of Troy and the Battle of Marathon.

Around 400 CE, the pictures were taken away by the Roman proconsul. We know this from information imparted by Bishop Synesius, who was greatly disappointed not to be able to view them during his visit to Athens. Bronze shields taken from defeated enemies were also displayed in the Stoa Poikile to remind Athenians of their former glories.

In contrast to many of the constructions of the Agora, the Stoa Poikile was a building of public use, albeit without any officials working within it. It was built and used as a lesche (a place for both relaxation and meetings). It should therefore be of little surprise that it attracted hordes of Athenians, including those whose activity demanded an audience, such as jugglers, sword and

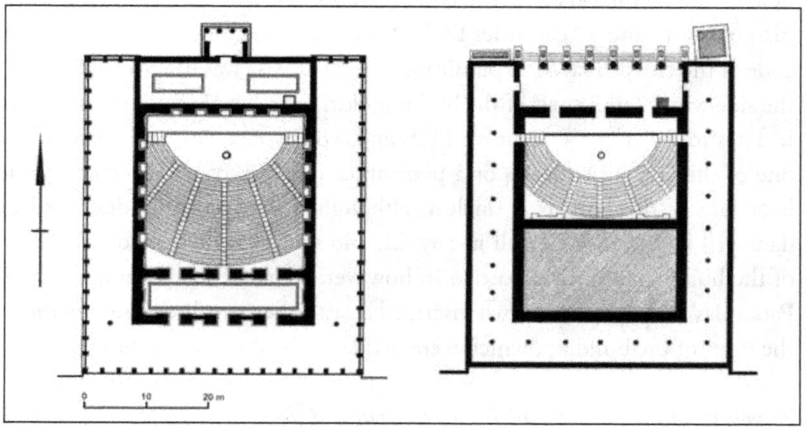

Plan of the Odeon of Agrippa: I – first phase (left), II – second phase (right) (after Thompson, Wycherley 1972, fig. 31).

fire swallowers and of course beggars. Philosophers were also amongst those who looked favourably upon the building, in particular Zeno, who came to Athens from Cyprus around 300 BCE and used the Stoa Poikile as his lecture theatre so often that both he and his followers were named 'Stoics'.

After passing through the entrance gate to the archaeological site, we first turn towards the massive statues of giants and tritons visible to our right, next to the former Panathenaic Way.

Before the entrance of the theatre which they call the Odeum (Music Hall) are statues of Egyptian kings. They are all alike called Ptolemy, but each has his own surname. (Pausanias: 1.8.6)

At the end of the 1st century BCE, a new building was erected within the Agora, the Odeon of Agrippa. The Odeon, which was a large concert hall, was funded by Marcus Vipsanius Agrippa (the son-in-law of Emperor Augustus), who visited Athens around 15 BCE.

It was a massive building on two floors (with measurements of 43.2 by 51.4 metres) and possessed a gabled roof covered in terracotta roof tiles. Its interior contained a twenty-metre high hall with an auditorium intended for around 1,000 people. The auditorium was separated from the fairly narrow stage (*pulpitum*) by a small orchestra with an altar in its central part. Behind the viewing area were further sizeable rooms.

Statue of a triton at the entrance to the Odeon of Agrippa.

The building was surrounded on three sides by a cryptoportico (an underground columned hall) on its lower level with a monumental Corinthian portico situated above. The façade of the building was formed by Corinthian pilasters. The Odeon could be entered from the south via the upper level of the central portico (the central stoa) or from the north through a small, four-columned portico on the ground floor.

The great auditorium eventually turned out to be too large and, in 150 CE, the roof of the Odeon collapsed. The building was then converted into a lecture theatre with the number of seats reduced to around 500, although the north façade was now significantly more elaborate, being as it was adorned with pillars presenting giants and tritons, as well as other forms of decoration.

The complex was destroyed by the Heruli (along with the most of the other buildings of the Agora) in 267 CE. At the beginning of the 5th century CE, it was rebuilt and included within a larger site, probably a palace, with several courtyards and numerous rooms and bathrooms. The statues of giants and tritons were then used to adorn the monumental entrance to the complex, hence their modern day positioning atop high pillars.

To the right (north) of the path which we are now proceeding westwards along, there is an empty space. A temple dedicated to the god of war, Ares, would once have stood here (to the north of the Odeon of Agrippa).

Near the statue of Demosthenes is a sanctuary of Ares, where are placed two images of Aphrodite, one of Ares made by Alcamenes, … (Pausanias: 1.8.4)

The erection of the Temple of Ares in this area dates to the Early Roman period, although the preserved marble sections of the building, which are currently situated in the western part of the square, date to the 5th century

The site where the Temple of Ares once rose.

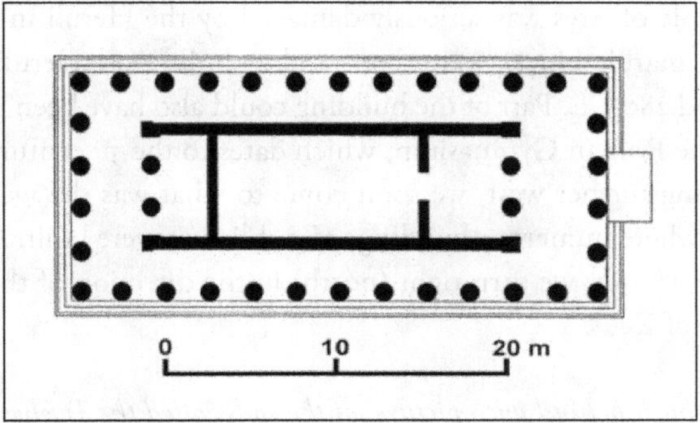

Plan of the Temple of Ares (after Thompson, Wycherley 1972, fig. 39).

BCE. This demonstrates that a peripteral, Doric temple, designed in the same manner and of the same size as the nearby Temple of Hephaestus, once stood here. Roman stonemason markings carved into the marble blocks, however, suggest that the temple was originally located elsewhere. It must therefore have been painstakingly taken down with all the parts being precisely labelled before being placed on new foundations within the Agora. We are dealing here with one of the best examples of a phenomenon termed 'temple wandering'. In the times of Roman dominion over Greece, many temples from the surrounding areas of Athens were dismantled and then rebuilt in the city centre in order to facilitate the construction of new temples, mostly dedicated to the deified emperors,. This was a fairly cheap and efficient way of propagating a new style of emperor cult. It is currently believed that the most likely origin of the Temple of Ares was the earlier Sanctuary of Athena Pallenis in the modern day village of Stavro, where the sizeable foundations of a Classical temple have been discovered without any trace of a construction on top.

The Temple of Ares was a typical Doric peripteros with six columns on its shorter and thirteen on its longer sides. The height of the columns reached 6.1 metres and the measurements of the stylobate were 16.76 by 36.25 metres. The cella of the temple was fronted by a pronaos and an opisthodomos was located at its rear. No trace of architectonic decoration has been discovered apart from sections of its acroterions. Pausanias mentioned two statues of Aphrodite, one of Athena and one of Ares standing within the temple, but they have not yet been discovered over the course of archaeological investigation. However, some researchers believe the marble remains which were found around the temple (currently on display in the Agora Museum) to have been the statues. A marble altar with measurements of 6.3 by 8.9 metres stood in front of the temple to its east.

The Temple of Ares was seriously damaged by the Heruli in 267 CE and some of its marble blocks were then used to build post-Herulian fortifications around 280 CE. Part of the building could also have been incorporated into the Late Roman Gymnasium, which dates to the 5th century CE.

Continuing further west, we soon come to what was the western side of the Agora, where numerous buildings of public use were built. After passing the Temple of Ares, we turn right (north) in the direction of the remains of the Portico of Zeus.

A portico is built behind with pictures of the gods called the Twelve. On the wall opposite are painted Theseus, Democracy and Demos. (Pausanias: 1.3.3)

The Stoa of Zeus was located in the western part of the Agora (currently to the south of the railway tracks). A small, Archaic chapel dedicated to Zeus probably initially stood here. Later, after the Battle of Plataea in 479 BCE, when the Greeks decisively 'freed' themselves from Persian 'occupation', an official cult place of Zeus Eleutherios (the Liberator) was established here.

Constructed in the years 430–420 BCE, the building (although it was dedicated to Zeus in memory of the earlier cult place) was not a typical temple. It took the form of a portico, but possessed certain new features from its time. To be exact, it was not a regular, oblong portico, although it did have two side wings which were positioned towards the front. It was built of limestone and marble, had Doric columns in its exterior and Ionic ones in the interior, all made of Pentelic marble. The measurements of the portico were 18 by 46.55 metres. According to Pausanias, it was decorated by paintings of Euphranor, a famous artist of the 4th century BCE. The shields of those who died while fighting for the liberation of Athens were also incorporated into the façade of the building.

South wing of the Stoa of Zeus.

Archaeological research conducted between the wings of the portico has also uncovered the remains of four statue bases. These were probably the sculptures which were mentioned by Pausanias in his description: Conon with his son, Timotheus, Evagoras, the king of Cyprus, Zeus Eleutherios and Emperor Hadrian. Of these, archaeologists have only discovered the statue of Hadrian (incomplete), which currently stands in front of the former Temple of Apollo. It is also worth paying attention to the magnificent armour of the emperor (which bears the image of Athena), two winged statues of Victory and a she-wolf feeding Romulus and Remus.

Statue of the Emperor Hadrian.

In the Early Roman period, two further rooms were built onto the back wall of the portico, which were probably used in the cult of the emperor's family. The building suffered badly during the invasion of the Heruli and elements of it were then used in building new constructions within the Agora in the 5th century CE.

Here is a picture of the exploit, near Mantinea, of the Athenians who were sent to help the Lacedaemonians. ... These pictures were painted for the Athenians by Euphranor, and he also wrought the Apollo surnamed Patrous (Paternal) in the temple hard by. (Pausanias: 1.3.4)

Not far to the south of the Zeus portico are the remains of the modest Temple of Apollo Patroos ('paternal', as Apollo was the father of Ion, the first of the Ionians, a group to which Athenians belonged). The temple is dated to the second half of the 4th century BCE. Earlier, in the Archaic period, there was only a small chapel dedicated to Apollo here. The foundations of the 4th century BCE building are nearly entirely preserved. At the front, the temple possessed four Ionian columns placed between antae (or, as recent research has indicated, six columns without antae). Via the vestibule, you came to the main room of the temple, a cella, with measurements of 8.64 by 9.28 metres.

The Temple of Apollo Patroos (in the foreground).

It was here that archaeologists came across the remains of what would have been the poros base of a cult statue of Apollo during their investigations. There was a small, adjacent room to the north of the cella with measurements of 4.4 by 4.56 metres.

A marble statue of Apollo Citharoedus

A monumental, marble statue was discovered in the vicinity of the temple, which researchers believe to be Apollo Citharoedus ('playing the cithara'). According to Pausanias, it was the work of Euphranor and it can now be found in the Agora Museum in the arcade of the Stoa of Attalos. The identification of the temple is certain thanks to Pausanias, who stated that is was located between the Stoa of Zeus and the Metroon, which lay to the south of the Temple of Apollo.

Here is built also a sanctuary of the Mother of the gods; the image is by Pheidias. (Pausanias: 1.3.5)

The Metroon. View from the North-East.

The Metroon performed two functions. It was both a sanctuary of the Mother of the Gods and the site of the city archive, where Athenian official documentation was stored. These documents were looked after by city slaves, who worked here as something like archivists. An official (*antigrapheus*) was also employed, who made copies of necessary documents for those requiring them.

The currently visible remains of the Metroon date to around halfway through the 2nd century BCE and are located on a site which contained earlier public buildings, including the Old Bouleuterion and a small temple of the Mother of the Gods.

The Hellenistic building consisted of four rooms of differing sizes, which were situated next to each other and fronted by a façade of 39 metres in length containing fourteen Ionian columns. Apart from a small section of the steps, all of the currently visible remains lay below ground level and formed part of the reddish stone foundations. The exact place where the documents were stored and where the statue of the mother of the gods,

Metroon (in the foreground). View from the West.

chiselled by Agoracritus (and not Phidias, as Pausanias mistakenly wrote), stood, is not known for certain. However, the statue most probably lay in the second room from the south (which would have thus performed the role of a small chapel) or in the north room (in the centre of a small columned courtyard). The remaining two rooms would have contained the city archive. The purpose of the building is no longer a matter of debate among researchers, as it is located exactly where Pausanias described it to be, namely between the Temple of Apollo Patroos, the Bouleuterion and the Tholos.

Farther up stand statues of heroes, from whom afterwards the Athenian tribes received their names. (Pausanias: 1.5.1)

On the other side of the path and opposite the Metroon are the remains of the Monument of the Eponymous Heroes. When the democratic system was introduced in Athens in 508 BCE, one of the reforms of Cleisthenes was to divide all Athenians into ten newly created tribes (*phylae*). 100 names of Athenian heroes were then sent to the Sanctuary of Apollo at Delphi, where the oracle chose ten of them to be the names of the tribes. Citizenship of Athens thereafter depended on belonging to one of these groups. The structure of the army was also based on contingents from different tribes and the city boule necessarily contained representatives of each.

The Monument of the Eponymous Heroes had a long, marble base. The bronze statues upon it were of the ten heroes of the tribes: Hippothoon,

The Monument of the Eponymous Heroes.

Plan and Reconstruction of the Monument of the Eponymous Heroes (after Travlos 1971, fig. 275).

Antiochus, Ajax, Leos, Erechtheus, Aegeus, Oeneus, Acamas, Cecrops and Pandion. It also served as a public notice board for citizens, whose names were hung on the high base below the appropriate tribe statue. Information which was given here included lists of those to be conscripted to the army and those to whom public honours were conferred, as well as proposed new legislation. The monument was surrounded by a stone perimeter with measurements of 3.68 by 18.4 metres and a height of around 1.5 metres. Only sections of the stone foundations, five of the limestone blocks of the base itself and two marble slabs (with their tops) have survived to our times.

Literary sources state that the statues of the Eponyms had already been created by 425 BCE. However, according to archaeologists, they must have been located in the south-west corner of the Agora at this time, as the monument which Pausanias admired could not have been constructed before 330 BCE. Research has also provided us with the knowledge that the monument was refurbished several times and that the changes in its appearance may have reflected the reorganisation of the faltering tribal system. We know that new phylae were created and that new heroes were added in Hellenistic and Roman times. The number of tribes (and of heroes) ranged between ten to a maximum of thirteen (the new heroes were Attalos, Ptolemy and Hadrian).

After familiarising ourselves with the Monument of the Eponymous Heroes, we now turn onto the path between the Metroon and the Temple

The Temple of Hephaestus. View from the South-West.

of Apollo. It leads westwards to the peak of a small hill (*Kolonos Agorajos*) on which the 'Hephaisteion' stands, one of the best preserved Doric temples in mainland Greece.

Above the Cerameicus and the portico called the King's Portico is a temple of Hephaestus. (Pausanias: 1.14.6)

The temple was built in the second half of the 5th century BCE and jointly dedicated to Hephaestus and Athena. It is a Doric peripteros made of Pentelic marble with six columns of 5.88 metres on the shorter sides and thirteen columns of the same height on the longer ones. The measurements of its stylobate were 13.71 by 31.77 metres and its interior consisted of three rooms: a pronaos, a cella and an opisthodomos. A two-floored colonnade stood along the side and back walls of the cella and bronze statues of Athena and Hephaestus by Alcamenes were placed within it.

The temple was very richly decorated. The metopes on the eastern side displayed the Twelve Labours of Heracles, whilst the northern and southern metopes presented the deeds of Theseus. It was due to the scenes featuring Theseus that the temple was for a long time known as the 'Theseion', a name

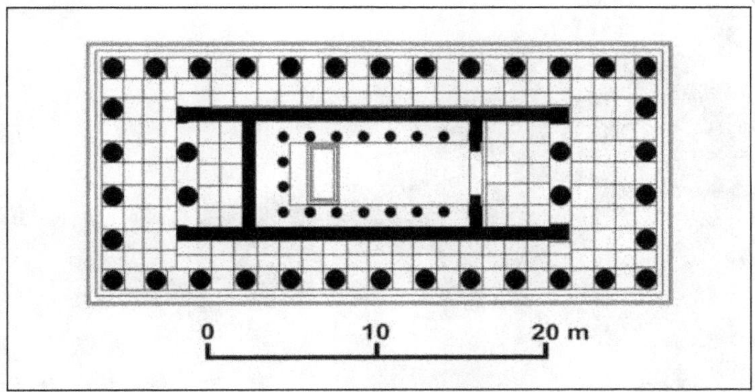

Plan of the Temple of Hephaestus (after Travlos 1971, fig. 335).

which has survived to our times as the name of an Athenian district and also the nearby metro station. Above the architrave of the pronaos and the opisthodomos was a continuous Ionic frieze presenting the Centauromachy and most probably battle scenes between the gods and the Cyclopes. The decoration of the gables depicted Heracles' admission into Olympus (on the eastern side) and the Centauromachy (on the western side). During excavation work conducted around the temple, the remains of a garden dating to the 3rd century BCE were also discovered. The Temple of Hephaestus was converted into a Christian church in the 7th century CE and it was this fact alone that saved it from later dismantling to obtain building material.

The area around the Hephaisteion offers wonderful views of the whole Agora, as well as the Acropolis which towers over it. We now continue our walk southwards along a small alley and then turn to the left (east) in the direction of the visible outline of the foundations of a round building, known as the Tholos.

Near to the Council Chamber of the Five Hundred is what is called Tholos (Round House); here the presidents sacrifice, and there are a few small statues made of silver. (Pausanias: 1.5.1)

The Tholos, which is recognisable even today thanks to its circular shape, served as the seat of the prytaneis. It was here that fifty senators, who changed every 35 or 36 days, were fed at the public's expense. At least seventeen of these would have spent the night in the building, in order to be able to counteract any kind of threat at any time. The Tholos was also the heart of democratic Athens, as it was the place in which the citizens serving others as senators could be found around the clock.

Tholos. In the background, on the left, is the site where the New Bouleuterion once rose.

Apart from its main function (Prytaneion), the Tholos was also the headquarters of the office of weights and measures, where official sample weights made of bronze could be found, as well as other objects.

Built in 470 BCE, the Tholos, which was bereft of decoration, possessed an entrance from the east. In its interior, which had a diameter of 8.45 metres, six columns held up a conical roof covered by large terracotta tiles. The floor was initially made of beaten clay, but, in the 2nd century CE, it was replaced

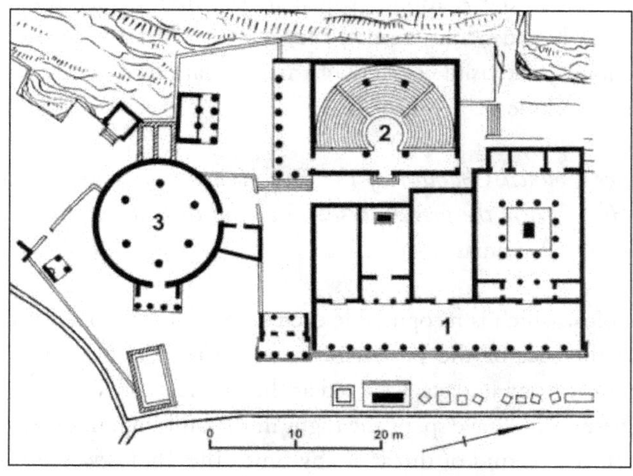

Plan of the south-west corner of the Agora: 1 – Metroon, 2 – New Bouleuterion, 3 – Tholos (after Thompson 1962, fig. 8).

by a parquet floor made of marble slabs. A small annex, which was probably a kitchen, was built onto its north-west side. The round shape of the building was not all suited to its basic function of a dining hall. It is therefore highly probable that the traditional Greek way of eating a meal whilst lying down was sacrificed here for seating on simple benches. Archaeologists have discovered wine jugs and cups marked as public property around the building amongst other objects.

Traces discovered by archaeologists have also suggested that the Tholos suffered serious damage in the Late Hellenistic period, perhaps at the hands of the invading army of General Sulla. The building was probably quickly reconstructed after these events, before a new monumental entrance was created in the form of a four-columned Ionic portico under the rule of Emperor Augustus. The Tholos was again destroyed at the end of the 3rd century CE (this time by the Heruli), but it was once again rebuilt. The end finally came after it collapsed of its own accord around 400 CE.

Hard by is the council chamber of those called the Five Hundred, who are the Athenian councillors for a year. (Pausanias: 1.3.5)

The Bouleuterion was found just behind the Tholos. This was the meeting place of the 'boule', the Athenian senate. 500 Athenian citizens were chosen by lots every year and met every day (except for holidays) to prepare notes for the deliberations of gatherings open to all Athenian citizens (Ecclesia), which took place on the Pnyx hill every ten days.

The Bouleuterion has barely survived. Only the scarcely visible outline of its walls, uncovered by archaeological excavation, remains. The building dates to the end of the 5th century BCE (probably between 416 and 409 BCE) and replaced an earlier building of the same type. This previous construction was built around 500 BCE and parts of it were later discovered in the Hellenistic Metroon.

The place chosen for the New Bouleuterion was directly to the west of the old building on a higher terrace, which was specially prepared by cutting into the rock of the hill slope. The building measured around 17.5 by 22.5 metres and the majority of it was taken up by a semi-circular auditorium, where the members of the boule would have sat. The southern section was formed by a seven-columned portico, through which it was possible to pass into a small courtyard. Similarly to many other buildings at the Agora, this bouleuterion was badly damaged by Sulla's army and then by the Heruli in 267 CE. After reconstruction in Late Roman times, the new building probably did not perform the same function as the earlier bouleuterion.

The Stoa of Attalos. View from the South.

We continue our walk to the east along the 'Central Portico' towards the reconstructed Stoa of Attalos II visible in the distance. This impressive portico stretches along the eastern edge of the Agora and was totally overlooked in Pausanias' description. Today, however, it is impossible to miss it. It was constructed at the behest of the leader of Pergamon, Attalos II (159–138 BCE), who had studied in Athens under the philosopher, Carneades, before becoming king. The stoa was predominantly a place containing shops with luxury

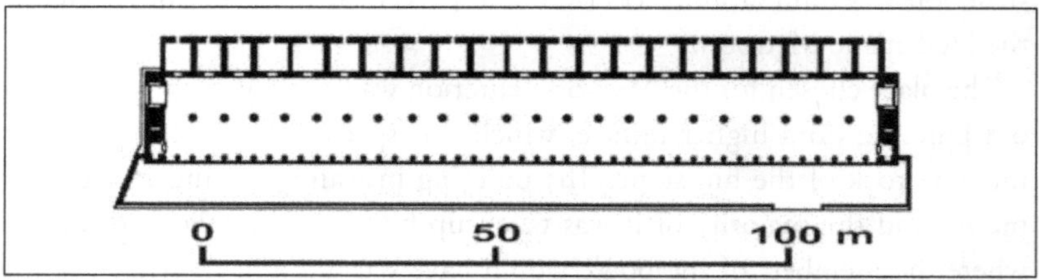

Plan of the ground floor of the Stoa of Attalos (after Thompson, Wycherley 1972, fig. 28).

goods. The double colonnade over two floors created a spacious passage for 42 shops, which were rented out by the city. Limestone, white Pentelic marble and blue marble from Mount Hymettus were used to construct the walls.

The Stoa of Attalos was the main trade centre of Athens for many years, before it was destroyed by the Heruli in 267 CE. Afterwards, it was incorporated into the new fortifications of the city. Between 1953 and 1956, the building was totally reconstructed by an American expedition working on the Agora site. It now houses the Agora Museum, which contains collections presenting the fruits of around eighty years of archaeological research on the site. Our visit to the Athenian Agora ends with a visit to this museum.

Herm found on the Athenian Agora.

Kerameikos

Kerameikos is the place where Pausanias began his visit to Athens. This is perfectly understandable considering the fact that the main gate of the city was located here, to which roads (including that from the Athenian port of Piraeus) led. Today, it should take no longer than one-and-a-half hours to see the whole excavation site and its small museum. The museum is a good place to start your visit, as objects found during excavations conducted on the site (mainly pottery) are collected here. Afterwards, a short stroll amongst the former tombs and then in the direction of the old Athenian fortifications (where the remains of the Sacred and Dipylon Gates are located) can be taken.

Along the road [to Athens – W.M.] are very famous graves, that of Menander, son of Diopeithes, and a cenotaph of Euripides. (Pausanias: 1.2.2)

Pausanias entered Athens from the Piraeus side through the famous Dipylon Gate, which is found in the area of Kerameikos. As stated

Pyxis with lid found on Kerameikos.

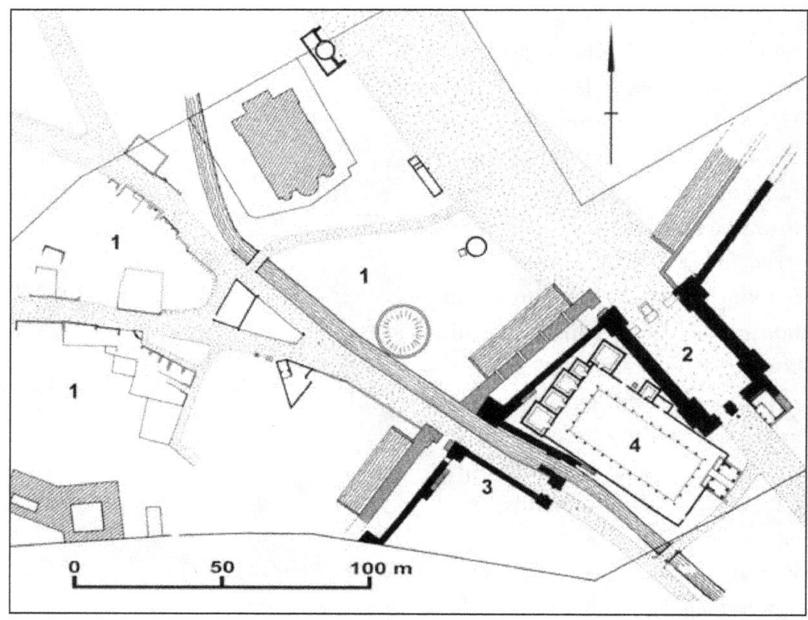

Plan of Kerameikos: 1 – Necropolis, 2 – Dipylon Gate, 3 – Sacred Gate, 4 – Pompeion (after Travlos 1971, fig. 391).

Grave steles at Kerameikos.

above, Kerameikos was one of the Athenian districts and was situated in the north-western part of the city. The name either comes from the pottery workshops (*kerameis*) which were located here or, as Pausanias has it, from the name of the hero, Keramos, the son of Dionysus and Ariadne. Within the limits of the city walls, the district stretched from the Dipylon Gate all the way to the Agora, which, according to Pausanias, also lay within its confines.

The most important Athenian necropolis (which is now also called Kerameikos) lay outside the walls of the city adjacent to the roads running towards Eleusis and Thebes.

It contained numerous marvellous tombs, as well as the *Demosion Sema*, the place where Athenians burnt the bodies of their dead heroes and citizens of merit. The necropolis, which was used for nearly 1,500 years, was divided into two parts by the riverbed of the river Eridanos. Excavation work on the Kerameikos necropolis was begun in 1870 by members of the Greek Archaeological Society. In 1913, German archaeologists took over and they are still working on the site today.

Dexileos stele (copy) at Kerameikos.

Following over 100 years of archaeological research, it has been established that the dead were buried here in simple pit graves in the Sub-Mycenaean period (around 1100–1050 BCE). In the Protogeometric period (around 1050–900 BCE), the first cremations occurred, which became the dominant trend, although inhumation was still carried out. The Geometric period (around 900–700 BCE) saw an increase in the affluence of Athenian citizens and alongside it the furnishing of their burials. Certain

The Tumulus of Eukoline at Kerameikos.

graves sometimes had large pottery vessels (kraters or amphorae) placed upon them and were decorated with scenes of funerals or the bewailing of the dead. In the Archaic period (around 700–480 BCE), round barrows (tumuli) began to appear, which were raised over the grave. They often had stone statues or bas-relief steles on top. Many of these objects were later used in construction work on the nearby city fortifications, which were erected in 478 BCE.

In the Classical period (480–323 BCE), a new trend in the necropolis was the building of rectangular fenced-off areas, within which the dead belonging to one family or clan was buried. Bas-relief steles were still placed on the graves of the dead, but great marble lekythoi or statues, sometimes presenting animals, now appeared. In the Hellenistic period (323–31 BCE), the graves of the dead were marked on the surface by small columns (*kioniskoi*) with the name of the deceased, their father and the demos from whence they came inscribed onto them. The site continued to be used as an area where citizens were laid to rest in Roman times.

After visiting the necropolis, we turn to the south in the direction of the remains of the fortifications of ancient Athens, which are now visible in the distance.

As you go up from the Peiraeus you see the ruins of the walls which Conon restored after the naval battle off Cnidus. For those built by Themistocles after the

The Sacred Gate (in the foreground to the right) and the Pompeion (in the background). View from the North.

The remains of the Dipylon Gate.

retreat of the Persians were destroyed during the rule of those named the Thirty. (Pausanias: 1.2.2)

The best preserved sections of the ancient walls of Athens can be found around two former gates, the Sacred Gate and the Dipylon Gate. The preserved length of the walls which have been dug up during excavation is around 175 metres. It is clear that the wall had a stormy history from the differing styles and variations it contains. Archaeologists have identified as many as six main phases of construction of the fortifications beginning in the first half of the 5th century BCE (the Themistocles Wall) and finishing with traces of repair and rebuilding in the 3rd century CE. The walls were on two levels. The lower was approximately one metre high and was made of regularly worked stone blocks, which created an inner and outer face. The space between them was filled by earth and stone rubble. The upper part of the wall was made of dried brick, faced by a layer of clay or plaster, in order to avoid the softening of the wall during rainfall. In its entirety, the wall was around eight to nine metres high. The stone base of the wall (the lower level) was raised every time that the wall was reconstructed (for example after its destruction during the Peloponnesian War or after the defeat in the battle of Chaeronea, when the Macedonians were preparing to attack the city), which accounts for the varied nature of the wall visible today.

In the first phase of construction of the Themistocles Wall, many wonderful funerary pieces from the nearby necropolis were used to create the stone base. Some of these were rediscovered during excavation and can now be admired at the National Archaeological Museum of Athens.

Due to an improvement in siege tactics, the need to build a second sequence of walls arose. At the end of the 4th century BCE, the interior wall (*proteichisma*) was therefore constructed, as well as a dry fosse of four metres in depth and eight metres in breadth preceding it.

The two gates were also found within this investigated section of the fortifications. Both were part of the Themistocles Wall, but underwent a series of changes in a later period.

The larger of these was the Dipylon Gate and, as the name implies, it was a double gate (*dipylou*). Initially, however, it was known as the Thriasian Gate. It was the main entrance to Athens and thus was designed to impress. The gate itself was positioned a little behind the line of the walls and this created a kind of courtyard in front of it. It was surrounded on three sides by a wall around nine metres in height and the corners of the courtyard all contained towers, which gave the entrance to the city additional protection.

The gate first possessed a stone (poros) base and the construction on top was of dried brick, in a similar style to the walls of the city. At the end of the 4th century BCE, the Dipylon Gate was, however, completely rebuilt and this time it was made of stone chippings faced by regular limestone blocks. In the Hellenistic period, an additional second pair of doors were built between the exterior towers.

City Wall next to the Sacred Gate.

The Sacred Gate (*hiera pyle*) guarded the road which led in the direction of Eleusis. It was built in the same way as the Dipylon Gate during the construction of the Themistocles Wall. Similarly to this gate, it possessed a rectangular courtyard at the front with corner towers to facilitate the defence of the city. A special channel of the river Eridanos also flowed through it. As was the case with the other city walls, the gate was rebuilt at the beginning and end of the 4th century BCE.

On entering the city there is a building for the preparation of the pro-

The Propylon of the Pompeion. View from the South-East.

cessions, which are held in some cases every year, in others at longer intervals. (Pausanias: 1.2.4)

At the beginning of the 4th century BCE, the Pompeion was built between the Sacred Gate and the Dipylon Gate. This complex consisted of a rectangular courtyard surrounded by a colonnade and six adjoining rooms to the north (two) and west (four), which were intended for the consumption of ritual meals. The courtyard was entered via a magnificent, marble propylon, which was located on its south-east side. It was precisely in this place that the famous Panathenaic Processions (*pompe*) took place. Before the procession began, the chosen Athenians (mainly priests and high-ranking city officials) attended a feast, during which the meat of sacrificed animals was consumed.

The Pompeion was destroyed by the Roman army of General Sulla in the 1st century BCE and was never rebuilt. In the 2nd century CE, a small basilica was constructed here and it remained in use until the invasion of the Heruli in the 3rd century CE. This was then replaced by two porticos in the 4th century CE.

The National Archaeological Museum

The National Archaeological Museum is another obligatory stop on any tour of Athens.

Zeus (Poseidon?) of Artemision.

It is the place where the most important archaeological objects discovered across the whole of Greece have been collected. The most valuable of these is a collection of objects discovered by Heinrich Schliemann in Mycenae and the central room in which it is contained is the starting point of our tour. The enormous amount of gold exhibits cannot fail to make an impression. Particular attention should be paid to the wonderful gold death masks, gold and silver vessels, a stone rhyton in the shape of a bull's head and bronze ceremonial daggers adorned with gold and silver decorations. Objects from prehistoric sites (from the Stone and Bronze Ages) are found in the rooms adjoining the Mycenaean collection. The most valuable of these collections is that of marble idols (including a man playing a harp) discovered by archaeologists on the Cyclades.

Afterwards, it is worth spending some time on the enormous collections of Greek art dating from the Archaic to the Hellenistic period. These include masterpieces such as the bronze Statue of Zeus (or Poseidon) by Artemision, the marble Statue of Diadoumenos (tying a fillet around his head) and the famous, marble Great Eleusinian Relief. The upper floor can then be visited with the most important room here being that with objects from the site of Akrotiri on Thera (Santorini), known as the Pompeii of the Aegean.

DAY 2:

Hadrian's Library

The second day begins at the Monastiriaki metro station, from whence the remains of the complex known as Hadrian's Library lie to the south. Although little of the library itself has survived to our times, it is possible to discern the outline of the first Christian church to be built within

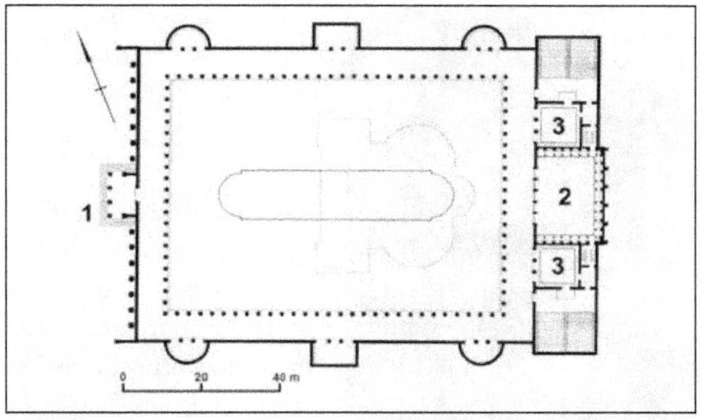

Plan of the Hadrian Library: 1 – Propylon, 2 – Library, 3 – Reading rooms (after Travlos 1971, fig. 316).

Athens in the place it once stood. A visit here should take no longer than half an hour.

... and, most famous of all, a hundred pillars of Phrygian marble. ... And there are rooms there adorned with a gilded roof and with alabaster stone, as well as with statues and paintings. In them are kept books. (Pausanias: 1.18.9)

The massive complex of Hadrian's Library is located to the north of the Roman Agora. It once boasted some of the most impressive architectural work of Athens and, at the same time, was a symbol of the cultural might of the city. The complex measured 82 by 122 metres and was made of limestone and different kinds of marble (including Pentelic and Phrygian). It was entered from the west via a small, protruding propylon with four Corinthian columns in its façade. This was flanked on the sides by a further fourteen Corinthian columns and the seven which lay to the north can still be admired in situ today.

Columns at the entrance to the Hadrian's Library complex.

The remains of the 5th century CE church in the middle of the complex of Hadrian's Library.

The library itself was located in the central room opposite the entrance and consisted of two storeys with recesses for wooden bookshelves. On the same wall (the eastern) of the complex, lektoria (reading rooms) could be found, as well as auditoriums. There was also an open courtyard with a garden and centrally positioned large swimming pool, which was surrounded by a wonderful portico of 100 columns (mentioned by Pausanias). The building was completed by apses and rectangular niches, which were found in the northern and southern walls. The complex was undoubtedly the cultural centre of Athens and its mighty walls ensured an oasis of peace and tranquillity was created within the bustling, noisy city.

The library was plundered and burnt during the Herulian invasion and parts of it were then incorporated into the new city fortifications. At the beginning of the 5th century CE, the inner colonnade and the rooms situated in the east of the building were then rebuilt by the Prefect of Illyria, Herculius. The remnants of a building with four apses visible within the complex are the remains of a church built around 425–420 CE, probably the earliest to be constructed in Athens.

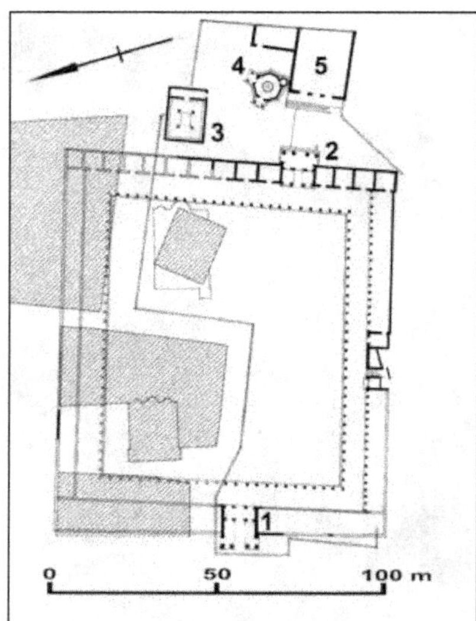

Plan of the Roman Agora: 1 – Gate of Athena Archegetis, 2 – Ionic Propylaea, 3 – Latrine, 4 – The Tower of the Winds, 5 – Sebasteion (after Travlos 1971, fig. 39).

The Roman Agora

On leaving Hadrian's Library, the remains of the Roman Agora now lie a little further to our south. They are found within the famous Athenian district of Plaka, which extends to the north of the Acropolis. This agora is worth a visit (if even for just a moment) for the former weather station which it contains, known today as the Tower of the Winds. Special attention should be paid to its reliefs presenting personifications of the eight winds. A visit here should take no longer than half an hour.

The Propylaea of Athena Archegetis.

Hadrian constructed other buildings also for the Athenians: a temple of Hera and Zeus Panhellenios (Common to all Greeks), a sanctuary common to all the gods, … (Pausanias: 1.18.9)

A temple to all the gods (*pantheon*) was built to the north of the Acropolis in the vicinity of the Roman Agora, although it was completely omitted from Pausanias' account of Athens. Unfortunately, the remains of the Pantheon are all now buried under modern buildings of the city.

The Roman Agora was a typical trade centre located around 100 metres to the east of the Agora itself and to the north of the Acropolis. The complex was built in the years 19–11 BCE and it measured around 98 by 111 metres. It consisted of a rectangular courtyard surrounded by Ionic porticos, the

The Roman Agora with the Ionic Propylaea in the foreground.

The Tower of the Winds.

easterly of which contained shops and warehouses, whilst the southerly possessed a small nymphaeum. There were two entrances to this agora. To the west stood a massive Doric propylaea, on which an inscription has been preserved. This informs us that the gate (and surely the whole complex lying behind it) was dedicated to Athena Archegetis ('Founder') and that it was raised thanks to a gift of the deified Gaius Julius Caesar and Emperor Augustus, his chosen son. To the east stood an Ionic propylaea. During the reign of Emperor Hadrian, in the 2nd century CE, the agora was paved with marble slabs.

The current entrance to the agora complex is found near to its north-east corner. The remains of a public latrine (built in the 1st century CE, probably during the reign of Emperor Vespasian) can be seen just next to the entrance. It was originally entirely covered by a roof except for the central vent and a water collecting system which allowed waste to be flushed out.

Just next to the latrine stands the wonderfully preserved building known as the Tower of the Winds, once called the House of Kyrrhestian. The founder and designer of the building was the famous Macedonian astronomer, Andronicus of Cyrrhus. The building was first and foremost a monumental clock (*horologion*); inside it was a water clock, whilst on the outside it was a sun clock. This octagonal tower, which was made of Pentelic marble and rose to a height of 12.8 metres, also performed the function of a weather station. Its walls were densely decorated on each side by bas-reliefs displaying personifications of the eight winds. According to ancient sources, a bronze sculpture of a triton was placed on the top to point in the direction that the wind was blowing. The construction of the Tower of the Winds dates to around 150–125 BCE, well before the Roman Agora was built.

The façade of the Sebasteion, a public building from the 1st century CE, lies to the south of the tower. It was dedicated to Athena and the deified Roman emperors (*Sebastoi Theoi*), amongst whom was most probably Claudius. The building is sometimes mistakenly called the Agoranomion (the office administering the market).

After visiting the agora and before heading in the direction of the next stop, the Olympieion, it is worth spending some time wandering the narrow streets of the wonderfully picturesque Athenian district of Plaka. The ancient Monument of Lysicrates, which stands between restored town houses, should not be overlooked. It is located within a small square at the western end of Lisikratous Street.

Leading from the prytaneum is a road called Tripods. The place takes its name from the shrines, large enough to hold the tripods which stand upon them, of bronze, … (Pausanias: 1.20.1)

Having visited the 'Roman' section of Athens, Pausanias then moved on in the direction of the southern slope of the Acropolis. The only construction to have survived to our times on the Tripod Road along which he would have walked is the Choragic Monument of Lysicrates, although it was not mentioned in his description at all. The Monument of Lysicrates consisted of a monumental base supporting a bronze tripod and was constructed in Athens in 334 BCE by the choragus, Lysicrates. Its high limestone platform bore a round rotunda with six half columns of Hymettian marble with panels of white, Hymettian marble placed in between them. An architrave in three parts ran above it containing bas-relief friezes depicting Dionysus turning pirates into dolphins. The whole construction was topped by a cornice and a steep roof, on top of which a richly adorned bronze tripod stood.

The Monument of Lysicrates.

The Olympieion

The Temple of Olympian Zeus lies to the south-east of the Acropolis within the boundaries of the former district of Athens built by the Emperor Hadrian. The entrance to the complex is now found in the vicinity of the tram stop, Zappio (Line 2: Syntagma-Voula). It is worth spending at least a little of your time here to witness just how mighty a temple the Olympieion once was. The preserved standing columns of the temple with their beautiful Corinthian capitals cannot fail to make an impression.

A visit to the Olympieion should be combined with a short walk to the now completely renovated Panathenaic Stadium, which lies around 400 metres to its east. Around an hour-and-a-half should be allotted to this combined trip.

Before the entrance to the sanctuary of Olympian Zeus ... stand statues of Hadrian, two of Thasian stone, two of Egyptian. (Pausanias: 1.18.6)

After familiarising himself with the Athenian Agora, Pausanias turned towards the south-eastern part of the city and headed in the direction of the 'District (or City) of Hadrian'. On the way, he passed other sites including the Gymnasium of Ptolemy, the Theseion, the Temple of the Dioskouroi and the Serapeion. The location of these buildings has not yet been determined by archaeologists, but in any case the most marvellous building of 'Hadrianopolis' was undoubtedly the mighty Temple of Olympian Zeus.

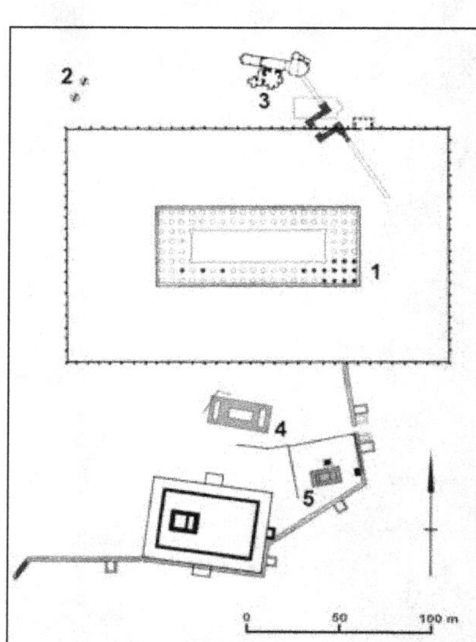

Plan of the Olympieion surroundings: 1 – Temple of Zeus, 2 – Arch of Hadrian, 3 – Roman bath, 4 – The Temple of Apollo, 5 – The Temple of Kronos and Rhea (after Travlos 1971, fig. 380).

The cult of Olympian Zeus must have lasted a considerable amount of time, as a small Doric temple already stood on the site of the current building as early as around 590–560 BCE. In 520 BCE, the family of the tyrant, Peisistratos, then began work on a new, monumental temple, over twice as large as its predecessor. It was planned that a Doric double colonnade would surround it, using the impressive Ionic temples at Ephesus

The Temple of Olympian Zeus – the Olympieion.

(in modern day Turkey) and on the island of Samos as its models. However, construction work on the temple came to an end when the tyrant fell from power.

King Antiochus IV Epiphanes of the Seleucid dynasty, who had spent several years in Athens as a youth, began the construction of a totally new temple in 174 BCE, albeit on precisely the same foundations as Peisistratos. The Roman architect, Decimus Cossutius, helped him in his work. The new temple adhered to the same design as the previous one, but this time Pentelic marble was used instead of poros rock and the order followed was Corinthian.

This temple, although it was not finished before Antiochus' death in 164 BCE, was to become one of the most admired in the Greek world of the age. In 84 BCE, however, it was partly dismantled and, along with pre-prepared elements intended to be used in later construction, was taken to Rome by General Sulla to be used as building material for the reconstruction of the Temple of Jupiter on the Capitol.

Further work on the Athenian Olympieion was carried out during the reign of Emperor Octavian Augustus, but it was to be Emperor Hadrian who completed construction of the temple. The consecration ceremony took place in the winter of 131 CE.

The new Olympieion possessed imposing measurements of 41.6 by 107.86 metres and was entirely made of Pentelic marble. Both of its facades consisted of eight columns in three rows and its longer sides contained twenty columns in two rows. Wonderful Corinthian capitals were designed specifically for this temple, which were nearly entirely covered in acanthus leaves. The interior of the temple contained a partially covered cella, in which two chryselephantine statues of Zeus and Hadrian stood, both of which Pausanias would later admire. Both also possessed their own altars. Various cities of the eastern part of the Roman world funded the production of tens of statues of Hadrian around the temple. Amongst the still visible remains, it is possible to see a base of one of these statues, which was paid for by the inhabitants of Koropissos (now located in southern Turkey).

In the 5th and 6th centuries CE, elements of the temple were used in the construction of a nearby church and the trend of removing parts from the temple continued up until halfway through the 18th century. Today, we can only admire its mighty platform and fifteen standing columns, topped by magnificent Corinthian capitals, which support the remains of the architrave.

The relatively modest Arch of Hadrian, which was once the entrance to Hadrian's District from the centre of Athens, stands in the vicinity of the Olympieion. The arch takes the form of a single-arched gate decorated with Corinthian pilasters. In its attic, further Corinthian pilasters are visible, as well as fluted columns supporting a small, triangular gable. Two inscriptions have been preserved on the architrave of the arch. The one to the west pro-

View from the Acropolis of the Arch of Hadrian, the Olympieion and the Panathenaic Stadium.

claims 'This is Athens, the ancient City of Theseus', whilst the one to the east 'This is the City of Hadrian, and not of Theseus'.

The City of Theseus was of course an old name for Athens, whereas the City of Hadrian was the name of a new district in Athens (including earlier buildings located within it) which lay to the south-east of the centre and was created thanks to the generosity of Emperor Hadrian. His arch and its surroundings would have undoubtedly been an element in the architectonic framing of the Olympieion.

Marble floor (opus sectile) in the apodyterium of the Roman Bath.

Between the Arch of Hadrian and the Olympieion are the remains of a section of the Themistocles Wall, as well as the Hippades Gate. The drum column visible here was reused in the building of fortifications, having previously been part of the unfinished Olympieion of Peisistratos. To the west of the fortifications, public baths from the times of Emperor Hadrian can be found, one of the best preserved examples of the type in Greece. They had the classic Roman layout, possessing an entrance room and a changing room (*apodyterium*), as well as cold (*frigidarium*), warm (*tepidarium*) and hot (*caldarium*) rooms. The baths were richly decorated with marble columns, statues placed in niches, multi-coloured stone parquet floors (*opus sectile*) and mosaics.

Close to the temple of Olympian Zeus is a statue of the Pythian Apollo. There is further a sanctuary of Apollo surnamed Delphinius. (Pausanias: 1.19.1)

During the previously mentioned archaeological excavation conducted to the south of the Olympieion, the remains of the foundations of a Doric temple from around 450 BCE (with measurements of 15.9 by 33.27 metres) were discovered. It has now been identified as the Temple of Apollo Delphinios (of Delphi).

A small Roman temple was also located nearby, which was probably the Temple of Kronos and Rhea (with measurements of 10.08 by 15.63 metres). It was mentioned by Pausanias and dated to around 150 CE. Both temples were destroyed during the building of new Athenian fortifications between 253 and 260 CE.

A marvel to the eyes, though not so impressive to hear of, is a race-course of white marble, … This was built by Herodes, an Athenian, and the greater part of the Pentelic quarry was exhausted in its construction. (Pausanias: 1.19.6)

To the east of the Olympieion lies the Panathenaic Stadium, wonderfully restored towards the end of the 19th century to mark the revival of the Olympic Games, which returned thanks to the efforts of Baron de Coubertain. The first Panathenaic Stadium was erected in the 4th century BCE, before Herodes Atticus entirely financed its reconstruction around 144 CE. The new construction was made of Pentelic and Hymettian marble and could hold as many as 50,000 people. Apart from the traditional athletic disciplines, it is possible that fights with wild animals also took place here. This could be indicated by the wall dividing the arena from the stands, as well as the Roman tradition of providing 'entertainment for the people'.

After the death of Herodes, Athenians organised a state funeral in his honour. Archaeologists have discovered a small altar near the stadium, which was dedicated to He(rodes), the hero of Marathon (Herodes Atticus was the owner of a sizeable residence not far from Marathon), which suggests that his grave may also be located in this area.

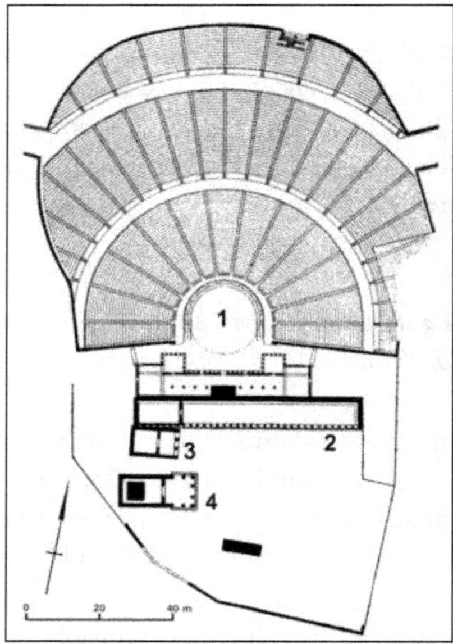

Plan of the Dionysus Theatre complex: 1 – Theatre, 2 – Stoa, 3 – Archaic temple of Dionysus, 4 – Temple of Dionysus from the 4th century BCE (after Dinsmoor 1975, fig. 77).

The Southern Slope of the Acropolis

The monuments lying at the foot of the Acropolis are often passed over by organised tour groups. This is a great pity, since they are certainly worth a visit. Two of them stand out, namely the Theatre of Dionysus and the Odeon of Herodes Atticus. The entrance to this site can be found virtually opposite the new Acropolis Museum on Dionysiou Areopagitou Street. It should take between an hour-and-a-half and two hours to complete your visit.

The oldest sanctuary of Dionysus is near the theatre. Within the precincts are two temples and two statues of

The Theatre of Dionysus with the new Acropolis Museum in the background.

Dionysus, the Eleuthereus (Deliverer) and the one Alcamenes made of ivory and gold. (Pausanias: 1.20.3)

The Theatre of Dionysus is located on the southern slope of the Acropolis. This was the earliest theatre of Athens, having been built in the 6th century BCE, and was therefore relatively primitive. The building did not contain a stone viewing area, meaning that the public had to sit directly on the slope of the elevation. Spectacles were performed on the small orchestra and the theatre also possessed a temporary stage building made of wood. In the 4th century BCE, the Theatre of Dionysus was completely rebuilt. A new stage building (*skene*) with measurements of 6.4 by 46.5 metres was then constructed, as well as a stunning auditorium. Within the orchestra, which had a diameter of nineteen metres, stood an altar (*thymele*) of Dionysus. The auditorium consisted of 64 rows of seating made of limestone and divided into thirteen sectors. An additional fourteenth sector was added when needed on the hill and thus, when full, the theatre could hold around 17,000 spectators. The first row contained honorary seats of Pentelic marble with back support (*proedria*) for important dignitaries. The most central of these was a throne intended for the highest ranking priest of Dionysus. The balustrade made of marble slabs in front of the first row was added in the 1st century CE, when the theatre started to be used for gladiator fights.

The stage building was rebuilt many times. In the Hellenistic period, a proskenion and paraskenia were added. It would then have been during renovation work in the 2nd century CE that the wonderful relief presenting the Greek gods and crouching images of Silenus was introduced underneath the stage building. Further decoration of the theatre was completed in the times of Lycurgus (the second half of the 4th century BCE) in the form of statues of famous tragedians, such as Aeschylus, Sophocles and Euripides.

Just next to the theatre are the remains of a portico built in the 4th century BCE and two small temples of Dionysus. The first temple, the foundations of which are visible next to the portico, was constructed in the 6th century BCE in a small templum in antis form. In accordance with tradition, a wooden statue of the god (*xoanon*) was brought here from Eleutherae, one of the traditional cult centres of Dionysus. The remains of the later temple, dating to the 4th century BCE, can be seen next to it. A chryselephantine statue of Dionysus would have been placed here, the work of Alcamenes, a student of Phidias. The temple consisted of a simple cella, which was fronted by a small pronaos surrounded on three sides by columns.

Near the sanctuary of Dionysus and the theatre is a structure, which is said to be a copy of Xerxes' tent. It has been rebuilt, for the old building was burnt by the Roman general Sulla when he took Athens. (Pausanias: 1.20.4)

Lying to the east of the Theatre of Dionysus, the Odeon of Pericles (currently not open to tourists), which Pausanias compared to the Tent of Xerxes in his description, was used for musical contests (including those of the Panathenaea). It was built around 440 BCE and was most probably modelled on the tent of the Persian leader, which is supposed to have been exhibited here previously as a spoil of war. In the times of Pericles, this enormous, square building (which is barely visible today) had sides of sixty metres and possessed a wooden roof supported by nine rows of columns. The Odeon of Pericles was not only used for musical competition, but was also a place where the court of Athens met and where lectures by famous philosophers were held.

The sanctuary of Asclepius is worth seeing both for its paintings and for the statues of the god and his children. (Pausanias: 1.21.4)

The cult of Asclepius was introduced relatively late in Athens (around 420 BCE) by a certain Telemachus, who must have come from Epidaurus. He erected a small sanctuary to the god on the southern slope of the Acropolis, which consisted of a holy spring, an altar and surrounding walls. It was here,

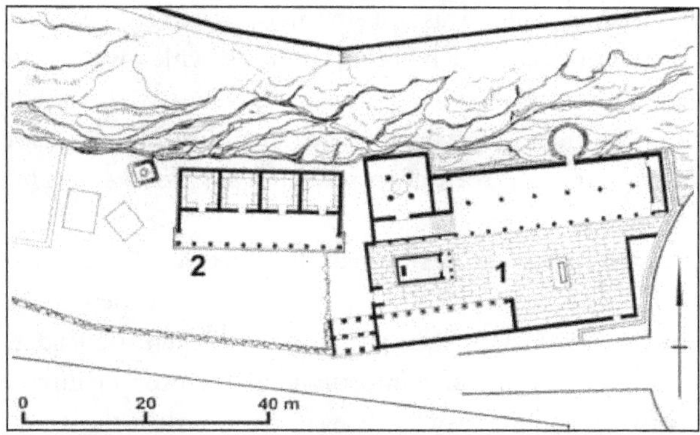

Plan of the temenos of Asclepius: 1 – Temple of Asclepius, 2 – Ionic portico (after Travlos 1971, fig. 171).

next to this spring, that Ares is supposed to have killed the son of Poseidon, Halirrhotius, a crime for which he was tried on a hill located to the north-west of the Acropolis. A small Ionic portico located to the west of the later temple perhaps also belonged to this early complex. It had four rooms to its rear, which were used for ritual feasting.

The temple itself and the new altar of Asclepius were built in the 4th century BCE after the Peloponnesian war. A two-floored Doric portico to the north of the temple courtyard was constructed at the same time. The portico would have been used as an abaton, a place where the sick were asked to dream, during which time the cure to their ailments would be mysteriously revealed to them.

On the western side of the slope is the partly restored Odeon of Herodes Atticus. Pausanias (7.20.3) informs us that Herodes built it around 160 CE in honour of his late wife, Regilla. The edifice possessed a mighty three-floored stage building

The Odeon of Herodes Atticus.

28 metres in height, which was once entirely coated by marble. Numerous statues filled the niches of the flanking columns, which were located behind the stage and opposite the viewing area. Marble was also used to lay the floor of the orchestra and the benches of the auditorium, which could hold around 5,000 spectators. The odeon probably possessed a roof made of precious cedar wood.

An impressive stoa once connected the Theatre of Dionysus with the Odeon of Herodes Atticus. It was one of the most expensive and famous constructions which Athens was gifted by the Hellenistic leaders of Pergamon, in this case Eumenes II. Unfortunately, the Stoa of Eumenes, which was built between 196 and 159 BCE, was destroyed in the 3rd century CE. Only a series of buttresses connected by semi-circular arches, which would have supported a terrace above, have survived to our times. It was clearly a two level structure and perhaps was designed by the same architect who was responsible for the portico of Attalos II in the Agora. The lower floor of the Stoa of Eumenes contained a Doric portico, whilst the upper was decorated with Ionic columns. It was intended to be a place of rest and shelter from the sun for the hundreds of Athenians taking part in theatrical performances and musical competitions.

On the eastern edge of the Eumenes portico (by the Theatre of Dionysus), the foundations of another wonderful choragic monument can be found. It was built by Nicias around 320 BCE and took the form of a small Doric temple. In the 3rd century CE, the monument was dismantled and used to build the Beulé Gate on the Acropolis.

The Acropolis Museum

The Acropolis Museum possesses the second most important collection of ancient Greek art in Athens after the National Archaeological Museum and is therefore most worthy of a visit. Most of the objects contained within come from the excavation of the Acropolis. Standing out amongst them are fragments of the architectonic decoration of the Parthenon (the majority of which, however, is currently in the British Museum in London) and wonderful examples of ancient Greek sculpture and reliefs, such as the Pensive Athena (relief), the marble kore, the Moschophoros and the Kritios Boy.

The Areopagus, the Pnyx and the Hill of the Muses

If you still have time and energy at your disposal after your visit to the museum, it is possible to stroll around the park located nearby, which extends as far as three important hills of ancient Athens. These are the Areopagus, the Pnyx and the Hill of the Muses. Entrance is free to each of them.

The Pnyx Hill. The place where the Ecclesia took place.

There is also the Hill of Ares, so named because Ares was the first to be tried here; ... (Pausanias: 1.28.5)

The limestone hill named the Areopagus, which lies to the north-west of the Acropolis, was dedicated to Ares and Erinyes. According to Pausanias (as mentioned above), it was the place where the god of war was tried for the murder of Halirrhotius and Orestes for the killing of his mother, Clytemnestra. In historical times, Athenians gathered here to deliberate, as it was then the site of the highest court of the city. From the 5th century BCE, the council was also known as the Areopagus, taking its name from the hill on which it was situated. Sessions probably took place on the north-eastern terrace of the hill, which lies directly opposite the Acropolis.

To the west of the Areopagus is the Pnyx hill, where meetings of all the adult citizens of Athens (the Ecclesia) took place. These were held on a specially prepared semi-circular terrace, the currently visible remains of which date to around 330 BCE. An imposing, semi-circular wall which once supported the auditorium has survived to our times. A rostrum was situated in the south of the auditorium and the Altar of Zeus Agoraios ('Protector of the Agora') was built above it in the 4th century BCE. Behind this altar, two sizeable buildings were constructed in the same period (probably porticos).

There is one more elevation to the north-west of the Acropolis, the Mouseion (the 'Hill of the Muses' – currently known as Philopappos Hill). In 294 CE, it was fortified by the Macedonian king, Demetrius I Poliorketes,

View from the Acropolis of the Odeon of Herodes Atticus and the Hill of the Muses (with the Monument of Philopappos on top).

but apart from the remains of walls at its peak, the relatively well-preserved funerary monument of the Roman, Gaius Julius Antiochus (dating to 114–116 CE), is the only site of interest to be found here.

PRACTICAL INFORMATION

Please note that it is possible to buy a special ticket which allows access to all of the archaeological sites mentioned in this guide for the price of 12 Euros (concessions – 6 Euros) at any of the individual ticket booths. This ticket does not, however, cover entrance to the National Archaeological Museum or the Acropolis Museum.

It should also be remembered that many people (from member states of the European Union) are entitled to free entry to the archaeological sites of Greece. This includes those over 65 or under 18, students and academic instructors.

It is always worth checking at the entrance about the possibility of a discount to the ticket price. A website prepared by the Greek Ministry of Tourism is also of assistance in this matter: http://odysseus.culture.gr/index_en.html

The Acropolis:
Address: *Dionysiou Areopagitou Street. Metro: Acropolis*
Open: *Monday-Sunday: 8 a.m. – 8 p.m. (5 p.m. in winter)*
Tickets: *Full – 12 Euros; Reduced – 6 Euros*
Free admission days: *6 March, 18 April, 18 May, 5 June, the last weekend of September, every first Sunday from November 1st to March 31st*

Site closed: *1 January, 25 March, Easter Sunday, 1 May, 25–26 December*

The Ancient Agora:
Address: *24 Adrianou Street. Metro: Thissio*
Open: *Monday-Sunday: 8 a.m. – 8 p.m. (3 p.m. in winter)*
Tickets: *Full – 4 Euros; Reduced – 2 Euros*
Free admission days: *6 March, 18 April, 18 May, 5 June, 28 October, the last weekend of September, every first Sunday from November 1st to March 31st,*
Site closed: *1 January, 25 March, Easter Sunday, 1 May, 25–26 December*

Kerameikos:
Address: *148 Ermou Street. Metro: Thissio*
Open: *Monday-Sunday: 8 a.m. – 8 p.m. (3 p.m. in winter)*
Tickets: *Full – 2 Euros; Reduced – 1 Euro*
Free admission days: *6 March, 18 April, 18 May, 5 June, 27 September, the last weekend of September, Sundays in the period between 1 November and 31 March, National Holidays*
Site closed: *1 January, 25 March, Easter Sunday, 1 May, 25–26 December*

The National Archaeological Museum:
Address: *44 Patission Street. Metro: Omonia or Victoria*
www: http://www.namuseum.gr/index-en.html
Open: *Monday-Sunday: 8 a.m. – 8 p.m.*
Tickets: *Full – 7 Euros; Reduced – 3 Euros*
Please note that it is possible to buy a special ticket which allows access to the National Archaeological Museum, the Byzantine Museum, the Numismatic Museum and the Epigraphic Museum for the price of 12 Euros (concessions – 6 Euros).
Free admission days: *6 March, 18 April, 18 May, 5 June, 28 October, the last weekend of September, every first Sunday from November 1st to March 31st*
Museum closed: *1 January, 25 March, Easter Sunday, 1 May, 25–26 December*

Hadrian's Library:
Address: *3 Areos Street. Metro: Monastiraki*
Open: *Monday-Sunday: 8 a.m. – 3 p.m.*
Tickets: *Full – 2 Euros; Reduced – 1 Euro*
Free admission days: *6 March, 25 March, 18 April, 18 May, 5 June, 28 October, the last weekend of September, every first Sunday from November 1st to March 31st*
Site closed: *1 January, Easter Sunday, 1 May, 25–26 December*

The Roman Agora:
Address: *Plaka. Metro: Monastiriaki*
Open: *Monday-Sunday: 8 a.m. – 3 p.m.*
Tickets: *Full – 2 Euros; Reduced – 1 Euro*
Free admission days: *6 March, 25 March, 18 April, 18 May, 5 June, 28 October, the last weekend of September, every first Sunday from November 1st to March 31st*
Site closed: *1 January, Easter Sunday, 1 May, 25–26 December*

The Olimpieion:
Address: *Vassilisis Olgas Av. Metro: Acropoli*
Open: *Monday-Sunday: 8 a.m. – 8 p.m. (3 p.m. in winter)*
Tickets: *Full – 2 Euros; Reduced – 1 Euro*
Free admission days: *6 March, 18 April, 18 May, 5 June, 27 September, the last weekend of September, Sundays in the period between 1 November and 31 March, National Holidays*
Site closed: *1 January, 25 March, Easter Sunday, 1 May, 25–26 December*

Southern Slope of the Acropolis:
Address: *Dionysiou Areopagitou Street. Metro: Acropoli*
Open: *Monday-Sunday: 8 a.m. – 8 p.m. (5 p.m. in winter)*
Tickets: *Full – 2 Euros; Reduced – 1 Euro*
Free admission days: *6 March, 18 April, 18 May, 5 June*
Site closed: *1 January, Easter Sunday, 1 May, 25–26 December*

The Acropolis Museum:
Address: *15 Dionysiou Areopagitou Street. Metro: Acropoli*
www: http://www.theacropolismuseum.gr/en
Open:
1 April – 31 October: Monday: 8 a.m. – 4 p.m.; Tuesday-Thursday, Saturday-Sunday: 8 a.m. – 8 p.m.; Friday: 8 a.m. – 10 p.m.
1 November – 31 March: Tuesday-Thursday: 9 a.m. – 5 p.m.; Friday: 9 a.m. – 10 p.m.; Saturday-Sunday: 9 a.m. – 8 p.m.; Monday: closed
Tickets: *Full – 5 Euros; Reduced – 3 Euros*
Free admission days: *25 March, 18 May, 28 October*
Museum closed: *1 January, Easter Sunday, Easter Monday, 1 May, 25–26 December*

The Temple of Hephaestus. South-east corner of the temple.

The Temple of Poseidon.

SOUNION

The site of Sounion lies on a cape of the same name, located in the south of Attica (Greece). The main attraction is the beautifully positioned Temple of Poseidon, the reason for its status as one of the most eagerly visited tourist locations of modern Greece.

Apart from the temple itself, it is also possible to see the remains of fortifications and bastions, the entrance gate to the sanctuary and traces of several rooms once used as dining halls and places to store votive offerings made at the temple.

Having said all of this, a major draw for the majority of tourists is also the unforgettable view of the surrounding area, above all of the sea.

On the Greek mainland facing the Cyclades Islands and the Aegean Sea the Sunium promontory stands out from the Attic land. When you have rounded the promontory you see a harbour and a temple to Athena of Sunium on the peak of the promontory. (Pausanias: 1.1.1)

Cape Sounion represents the southernmost tip of Attica. At its peak, just next to the rocky seashore, a sanctuary of Poseidon was once found, as well as a small settlement surrounded by mighty defensive walls located next to it. A little further to the north, on one of the lower elevations, was a sanctuary dedicated to Athena and a small cult district made in honour of the hero, Frontis.

It was at Cape Sounion that Pausanias began the description of his wanderings around Greece. It is interesting that he named it the site of the Temple of Athena and not of the much better known Temple of Poseidon. Perhaps Pausanias' error was caused by the fact that the earlier Temple of Athena had been taken down and moved to the Athenian Agora in the 1st century CE. As a result, when he visited, the Temple of Poseidon was the only temple present on the site and the fact that its importance had diminished by the 2nd century CE was probably the reason he mistook it for the temple of the Attic patron goddess, Athena.

Cape Sounion was first mentioned in the Odyssey as the place where Frontis, the quartermaster of the ship returning with Menelaus from Troy, was shot by Apollo, died and was buried. Homer described Cape Sounion as a 'holy' place, perhaps because a sanctuary of Athena or Poseidon was located here in his times. Merchants or sailors crossing the Aegean Sea would have prayed here for a safe return journey or to give thanks for a successful voyage.

The area around Cape Sounion was settled in around 3000 BCE, which is attested by the presence of a prehistoric burial ground nearby discovered

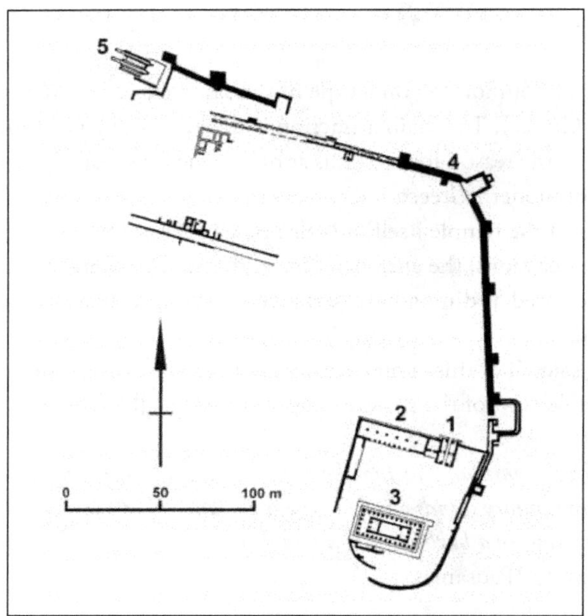

Plan of the Sanctuary of Poseidon: 1 – Propylon, 2 – North Stoa, 3 – Temple of Poseidon, 4 – Fortifications, 5 – Shipsheds (after Dinsmoor 1970, p. 1).

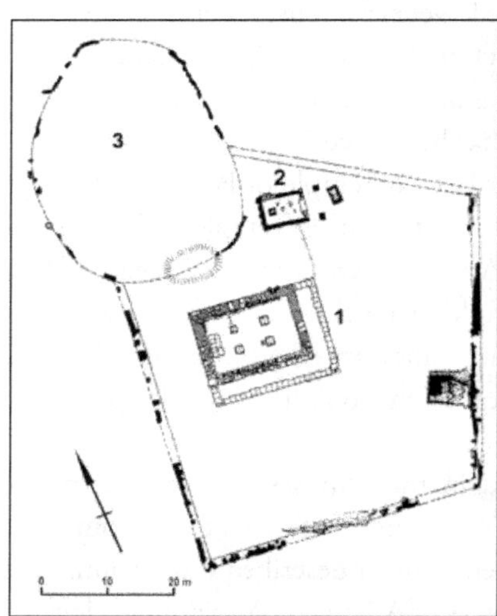

Plan of the Sanctuary of Athena: 1 – Temple of Athena, 2 – Archaic Temple of Athena (Artemis?), 3 – Precinct of Frontis (after Davaras 1979, fig. 12).

by archaeologists. Research has also shown that a cult was in existence within the area of the sanctuary from as early as the 8th century BCE. Near the later Sanctuary of Athena, a deposit in the shape of a fifteen metre rectangular pit was discovered, amongst other finds. It was filled with objects dating to the Early Archaic period and was probably a votive offering made within the holy precinct of Frontis. Amongst these objects were terracotta figurines and tiles, seals, scarabs and small Corinthian aryballoi. On one of the terracotta tiles dated to the 8th century BCE was a painted depiction of a warship with the quartermaster clearly highlighted. This may have been Frontis himself.

A series of marble kouroi statues were set in place within the Sanctuary of Poseidon at the beginning of the 6th century BCE. Archaeologists later found them in a pit to the east of the temple. One of them, which was over three metres high, can now be found in the National Archaeological Museum of Athens.

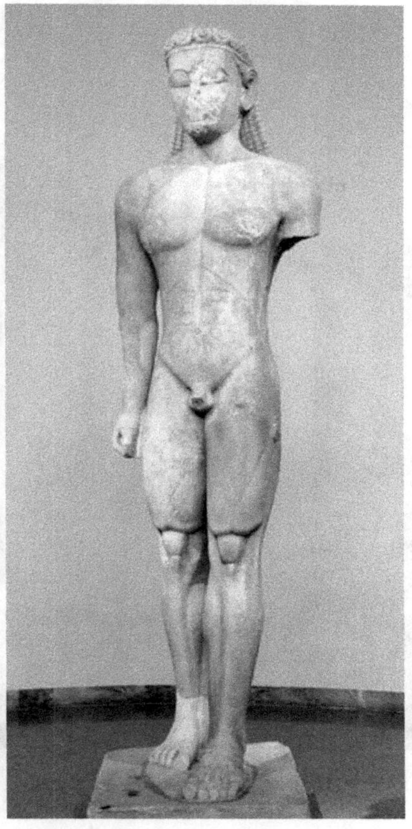

Kouros from Sounion (now in the National Archaeological Museum in Athens)

At the end of the 6th century BCE, a small temple was erected with two columns in its pronaos in the Athena precinct. Its interior contained a statue, the limestone base of which has survived to our times. In front of the temple, a small altar was located. It is not known to whom this early temple was dedicated. Apart from Athena, researchers suggest the possibility of Artemis amongst others.

Shortly after 500 BCE, the first Temple of Poseidon started to be constructed at the peak of the cape. It was of a similar layout and appearance to the later temple, the remains of which we can still see today, although it was somewhat smaller. The planning and construction of the temple was probably financed by Athens rather than the local demos (municipality) of Sounion. Sections of architectural detail of this earlier construction, including column drums, blocks of wall and Doric capitals, can be seen in the foundations of the later temple and were also used in the building of the Temple of Athena in the 5th century BCE.

Construction work was probably still ongoing when the Persians plundered the Sanctuary of Poseidon in 480 BCE and destroyed the emerging temple. Soon afterwards, following the battle of Salamis, the Greeks redressed the balance by seizing Phoenician warships as trophies to revenge themselves for this sacrilegious and barbarous act. It was only in the second half of the 5th century BCE, probably around 440 BCE, that the new

The Temple of Poseidon.

Temple of Poseidon was constructed. Somewhat earlier, around 460–450 BCE, a new temple was built in the Sanctuary of Athena. The Temple of Poseidon was made of local marble from the quarries of Agriles, which was quite rugged and soft, but attractively illuminated by coloured veins. The measurements of the stylobate were 13.4 by 31.15 metres, whilst the peristasis contained six columns on the shorter sides and thirteen on the longer. An

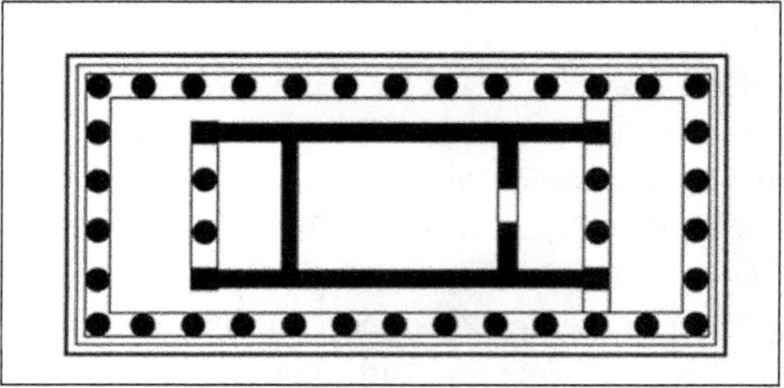

Plan of the Temple of Poseidon (after Dinsmoor 1970, p. 38).

interesting fact is that the slender, Doric columns contained only sixteen rather than the usual twenty grooves. One theory suggests this is because it made the columns appear more in proportion when viewed from the sea. It is also unusual that the columns of the pronaos were positioned in line with the third columns on the sides of the longer peristasis (typically they were in line with the second). This is also the case with the Temple of Ares and the Temple of Hephaestus in the Athenian Agora, as well as the Sanctuary of Nemesis at Rhamnous. Perhaps the same anonymous architect could have been at work on all these sites.

The interior of the temple consisted of a pronaos, cella and an opisthodomos to the rear. The walls were built of alternating rows of worked stone blocks of 0.3 and 0.6 metres in height (so-called 'pseudo-Isodomic' masonry). A continuous frieze of Parian marble (from the island of Paros) ran along the columns of the pronaos and presented battles between the gods and the giants (the gigantomachy), the Lapiths and the centaurs (the centauromachy) and the hunt for the Calydonian Boar. It was additionally decorated by sculptured gables, although we do not know which scenes were depicted on them. No ancient description of the cult statue of Poseidon that must have once stood in the cella has survived to our times.

The temple was placed within a temenos. It was entered through an imposing Doric propylon in the dystilos-in-antis style. Just next to the propylon were rooms with asymmetrically positioned entrances containing eleven benches, which were probably used to consume ritual meals. Further on, to

The remains of the monumental gateway to the Sanctuary of Poseidon.

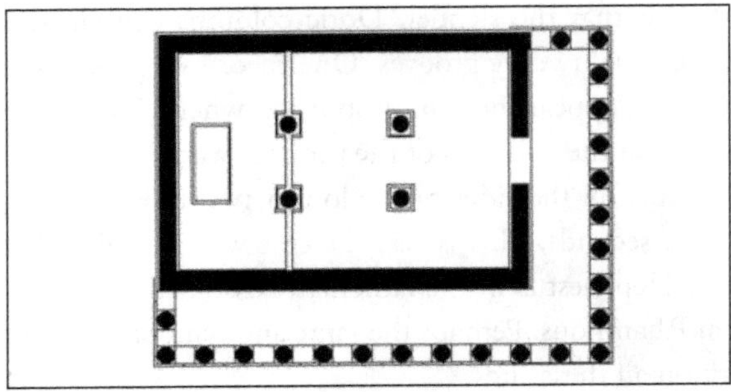

Plan of the Temple of Athena (after Davaras 1979, fig. 25).

the west of these rooms, were two Doric porticos, which would have held votive offerings made to the temple.

The Temple of Athena, which was located in a nearby sanctuary, was made of local marble (also from the quarries of Agriles) in the Ionic style and was probably one of the earliest Ionic constructions to be built on Greek territory. It belonged to the group of so-called 'irregular temples' mentioned by Vitruvius and measured 11.6 by 16.4 metres. It had a peristasis only on its eastern (ten columns) and southern (twelve columns) sides. The colonnade to the east would have formed the decorated entrance to the temple, whilst the one to the south could have served as a stoa giving shade on hot days and providing protection from the powerful winter winds. The interior of the temple contained only one room, the cella, which contained a statue of the goddess. The roof of the cella was supported by four columns. The

The location where the Temple of Athena once stood.

The Temple of Poseidon in the sunset.

foundations of the temple can still be seen in the centre of the sanctuary, but the temple itself (as was mentioned previously) was dismantled in the 1st century CE and used to construct the 'South East Temple' of the Athenian Agora. The marvellous base, which once would have supported the statue of Athena, has survived to our times. The same is also true of one of its Ionic capitals, which was used again in Athens and can now be viewed in the Athenian Agora Museum.

In the winter of 413/412 BCE, the Athenians fortified Cape Sounion in order to strengthen the defence of the sea route running in its vicinity. After subjugating Greece, the Macedonians extended the fortifications in the 3rd century BCE by adding an imposing bastion of marble blocks amongst other things. From this bastion, it is now very easy to see the line of fortifications from the 5th century BCE, which run first to the north and then to the west.

The Macedonians also constructed ramps and covered protection for ships in the north-western part of the promontory. The two ramps descended to the sea at a fairly steep angle and most likely would not have been intended for larger vessels, such as the trireme.

During a slave rebellion between 104 and 100 BCE, Sounion was the rebel base, from whence they carried out plundering raids on the Attica area.

After this period, the cape lost its importance. The Temple of Athena was taken down and used to make a new one at the Athenian Agora. As mentioned above, this was the probably the cause of Pausanias' mistake, which was not corrected until the end of the 19th century, when research excavations began. In 1884, these were led by the famous German archaeologist Wilhelm Dörpfeld and then between 1899 and 1915 by Valerios Stais on behalf of the Greek Archaeological Society. From this time onwards, the Temple of Poseidon has come to be recognised as one of the most romantic ancient Greek ruins. It has been visited and immortalised by artists such as William Turner and also Lord Byron, who carved his name into one of its columns.

PRACTICAL INFORMATION:

It is very straightforward to reach Sounion either by car or by local bus (including those serving Athens). This should bring you to the site in around one to one-and-a-half hours from the centre of the capital. It is easiest to travel here directly from Athens along the 'Attiki Odos', a road which covers the west coastline of Attica. However, Sounion can also be reached from the east coast of Attica by travelling through Lavrio.

After arriving at the car park (where the bus also stops), you should head to a path leading towards a restaurant building. To its west is the trail which leads to the archaeological site.

After walking alongside the old fortifications, you then cross them near a Hellenistic bastion before coming to the former entrance gate to the Sanctuary of Poseidon. To the west (right) of the gate, it is possible to see the foundations of rooms which were probably used for dining. Further on from them was a portico, where votive offerings made at the temple were placed.

Whilst walking around the temple itself, attention should be paid to the large amount of graffiti scratched into it by 'tourists', which includes the work of a certain Lord Byron.

After visiting the Sanctuary of Poseidon, it is then possible to descend to the former Sanctuary of Athena. In order to reach the site, one of the many paths leading off to the east (right) just after exiting the car park to the north should be taken. The Temple of Athena once stood on the small terrace to which these paths lead.

The best time of day to visit Sounion is in the early morning, before ten o'clock, as after this time many coach tours appear on the scene. However, Sounion is famed for its colourful sunsets and a visit here could therefore be combined with a trip to other locations within Attica such as Marathon and Brauron. Beginning such a trip by travelling from Rhamnous or Marathon south down the east coast of Attica, the day could thus be rounded off with a wonderful sunset in Sounion.

Sanctuary of Poseidon:

Open: *1 April – 31 October: Monday-Sunday: 8 a.m. – sunset*
1 November – 31 March: Monday–Sunday: 9:30 a.m. – sunset
Tickets: *Full – 4 Euros; Reduced – 2 Euros*
Free admission days: *6 March, 18 April, 18 May, 5 June, 28 October, the last weekend of September, every first Sunday from November 1st to March 31st, National Holidays*
Site closed: *1 January, 25 March, Easter Sunday, 1 May, 25–26 December*

It should be remembered that many people (from member states of the European Union) are entitled to free entry to the archaeological sites of Greece. This includes those over 65 or under 18, students and academic instructors.

It is always worth checking at the entrance about the possibility of a discount to the ticket price. A website prepared by the Greek Ministry of Tourism is also of assistance in this matter: http://odysseus.culture.gr/index_en.html

Sanctuary of Athena:

Open-air site. Permanently open.

The Treasury of the Athenians.

Many and different are the stories told about Delphi, and even more so about the oracle of Apollo. For they say that in the earliest times the oracular seat belonged to Earth, who appointed as prophetess at it Daphnis, one of the nymphs of the mountain. (Pausanias: 10.5.5).

Delphi is, without doubt, one of the most important archaeological sites of Greece. Visited by a huge amount of people in both ancient and modern times, it lies in a beautiful location on the southern slope of Mount Parnassus. Ancient Greeks believed that Delphi was the central point of the entire world, which can be confirmed by a symbolic stone standing in the Sanctuary of Apollo known as the 'Navel of the World' (*omphalos* in Greek).

Many different theories concerning the mythical beginnings of Delphi existed amongst ancient Greeks. Pausanias relates to us that it was the goddess of the Earth, Gaia, who was the first to rule the place. She then passed it on to Temida, the goddess of justice, who in turn offered it to Apollo.

They say that the most ancient temple of Apollo was made of laurel, the branches of which were brought from the laurel in Tempe. This temple must have had the form of a hut. The Delphians say that the second temple was made by bees from bees-wax and feathers, and that it was sent to the Hyperboreans by Apollo. (Pausanias: 10.5.9)

Pausanias describes the beginnings of the cult of Apollo at Delphi in an extremely colourful manner. Archaeologists agree with him in so far as they believe it must date to very ancient times indeed. Excavations carried out at Delphi have shown that the place was already settled in the times of the Mycenaean civilisation. The oldest remains, which come in the form of chamber graves, pottery and terracotta figures, date to approximately 1400 BCE and were discovered between the later Sanctuary of Apollo and the Cast-

The marble Omphalos at Delphi Museum.

alian Spring. Researchers suppose that the settlement was located within the surroundings of the sanctuary and that a Mycenaean cult centre, most probably in honour of the goddess Gaia, existed on the later site of the Sanctuary of Athena Pronaia ('forethought'). The Mycenaean settlement and sanctuary were destroyed by a fire, which would have been begun by the rubbing together of stones.

It is no wonder that the third temple was made of bronze, ... Some say that it fell into a chasm in the earth, others that it was melted by fire. ... The fourth temple was made by Trophonius and Agamedes; the tradition is that it was made of stone. (Pausanias: 10.5.11–13)

The beginnings of the cult of Apollo at Delphi date to the Geometric Period. From this time onwards, the fame of both the sanctuary and the oracle performing here spread across the whole known world. In the period of Greek colonisation, beginning in the 8th century BCE, the oracle at Delphi played the main role of guide and advisor to its expeditions. It should therefore come as no surprise that many new colonies were dedicated to Apollo with the moniker Archegetes ('Founder').

The sanctuary and oracle remained under the control of the local community until the beginnings of the 6th century BCE, when the 'Delphic Amphictyony' was created. This was a federation of twelve Greek tribes from Attica, Euboea, central Greece and the Peloponnese, who were to jointly rule the complex. One of the first decisions of the Amphictyony was to cre-

The Temple of Apollo.

The Sanctuary of Apollo. View from the entrance.

ate the new Pythian Games, which were to take place every four years from 582 BCE.

In the 6th century BCE, Delphi was at the peak of its development and many Greek cities established treasuries here at this time. The esteem in which the oracle was held rose to such an extent that even leaders of foreign countries sent numerous gifts and emissaries with questions concerning their own futures. One of these was the famous king of Lydia, Croesus, one of whose gifts was the statue of a gold lion, standing on a plinth made of electrum (a gold and silver alloy) and weighing 250 kg in its entirety. In exchange for this and other gifts, Croesus wished to obtain information on what would occur if he were to attack the mighty Persia. The reply of the oracle was: *A great empire will fall!* Croesus, believing that the oracle meant Persia, declared war. However, he was defeated and his whole empire fell soon after, proving the oracle correct!

In 548 BCE, the Temple of Apollo burnt down. Its reconstruction, which was completed in 510 BCE, was financed by a rich Athenian family, the Alcmaeonids, who had been chased out of Athens by the Peisistratids. During the Persian wars, the priestesses of Delphi tried to remain neutral and ordered many Greek cities, including Argos, to follow suit. However, the oracle ordered the Athenians to defend themselves with 'wooden walls'. This helped to convince Themistocles to build a powerful war fleet, thanks to which they defeated the Persians in a sea battle off the coast of the island of Salamis in 480 BCE.

After the Persian wars, Delphi retained its important status as many Greek cities erected further monuments and buildings here to thank Apollo for either rescuing them from or granting them victory over Persia. The most stunning of these monuments was built after the victorious battle of Plataea (479 BCE). It was a gold tripod placed on a bronze column in the form of three entwined snakes. The tripod itself was spirited out of Delphi during the so-called 'Second Holy War' (448–421 BCE), whilst the bronze column can now be admired at the former hippodrome of Istanbul (Turkey).

In 373 BCE, the Temple of Apollo was again destroyed, this time as the result of an earthquake that caused the rocks to alter their position. Despite immediate measures being taken to re-erect it, it still took forty years to complete and in the meantime, two further holy wars took place. The 'Fourth Holy War', which began in 339 BCE, led to the subjugation of all of Greece by Philip II of Macedon after the battle of Chaeronea in 338 BCE. Several years later, in 330 BCE, a new Temple of Apollo was consecrated at Delphi.

It seems that from the beginning the sanctuary at Delphi has been plotted against by a vast number of men. ... It was fated too that Delphi was to suffer from the universal irreverence of Nero, who robbed Apollo of five hundred bronze statues, some of gods, some of men. (Pausanias: 10.7.1)

In the 3rd century BCE, the sanctuary at Delphi fell under the control of the Aetolian League, thanks to which it avoided destruction during the Gallic invasion of Greece in 279 BCE. In 191 BCE, the Romans took control of the sanctuary. Although it continued to function, its golden years were already past. In 86 BCE, the sanctuary and its treasuries were looted by the army of General Sulla and three years later the temple was burnt down during an invasion by Thracians. Even Emperor Nero, a great lover of Greek art, plundered Delphi and made off not only with valuable treasure, but also with numerous statues (with which he planned to decorate his new palace in Rome). However, in 90 CE, Emperor Domitian rebuilt the Temple of Apollo and many other buildings. Hadrian, Septimus Severus and Caracalla were later to follow his lead.

The end of the sanctuaries of Delphi came in 394 CE after a decree by the Christian Emperor Theodosius I that prohibited adherence to the old 'pagan' beliefs. A small Christian community continued to function here for about another 300 years, but in the 7th century CE, the site was completely abandoned. In a later period, the small village of Kastri came into being on the site of what was once the Sanctuary of Apollo.

The first archaeological research of Delphi was begun in 1840 by German researchers and in 1891 the archaeologists of the French School of Archaeology in Athens were given permission to start investigating here. In order to begin the excavation, it was first of all necessary to move the whole village of Kastri, including its residents, to another place. Only after this had been completed was it possible to begin uncovering the remains of the sanctuary itself. Since then, archaeological excavations have been conducted at Delphi all the way up to the present day (with some short interruptions). The pieces discovered are now exhibited at the highly recommended Archaeological Museum, which was erected at the entrance to the site of the Sanctuary of Apollo.

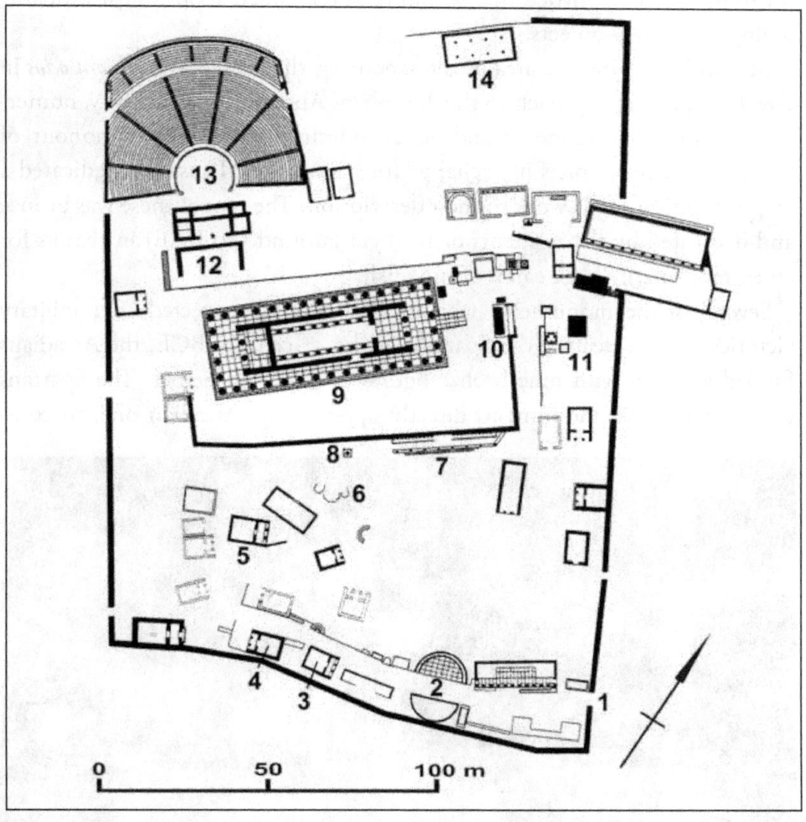

Plan of the Sanctuary of Apollo: 1 – Entrance, 2 – Exedrae of Argos, 3 – Treasury of the Sicyonians, 4 – Syphnian Treasury, 5 – Treasury of the Athenians, 6 – Rock of the Sibyl, 7 –Stoa of the Athenians, 8 – Column and Sphinx of the Naxians, 9 – The Temple of Apollo, 10 – The Altar, 11 – Tripod of Plataia, 12 – Ex-voto of Craterus, 13 – Theatre, 14 – Lesche of the Cnidians (after Poulsen 1920, Fig. 7).

The Sanctuary of Apollo

The city of Delphi, both the sacred enclosure of Apollo and the city generally, lies altogether on sloping ground. (Pausanias: 10.9.1)

The Sanctuary of Apollo was surrounded by a wall, the beginnings of which date to the 6th century BCE. The wall enclosed an area resembling a trapezoid in shape of approximately 135 by 195 metres at its widest.

The main entrance to the sanctuary is now found at its south-eastern corner, as it was in antiquity. Just in front of it are the preserved remains of the 'Roman Agora'. This is a small, rectangular, paved square, closed off to the north by an Ionic portico that would have contained shops, most probably selling devotional objects.

Just after entering the area of the sanctuary, the Sacred Way (*hiera odos* in Greek) begins its approach to the Temple of Apollo. Along the way, numerous treasuries, monuments and votive offerings were built in honour of the god by Greek poleis in exchange for his support. Pausanias dedicated a lengthy section of his work to their description. The first of these was bronze and dedicated by the residents of Korkyra (around 580 BCE) in thanks for an extraordinarily large catch of tuna fish.

Several of the monuments which followed it were erected after military victories. After defeating the Spartans in the 4th century BCE, the Arcadians funded a plinth with nine bronze figures of gods and heroes. The Spartans erected their own monument, directly opposite the Arcadian one, to com-

The 'Roman Agora' and the entrance to the Sanctuary of Apollo.

memorate their victory over the Athenians in the sea battle of Aegospotami in 404 BCE. It was a rectangular building with eight columns in the façade, containing 37 bronze statues presenting several gods, as well as the Spartan generals and admirals who presided over the victory. Right next to it was the bronze statue of a horse offered by the residents of Argos after their victory over Sparta in 414 BCE and next to this was another, also funded by Argives, to commemorate their victory over Sparta in the battle of Oenoe in 456 BCE. This monument presented the 'Seven Against Thebes', mythical Argive heroes.

Directly opposite the Argive monuments stood a votive offering of the Athenians, built after their victory over the Persians in the battle of Marathon. It included statues of Athena, Apollo, General Militiades and seven Athenian heroes, all sculpted by Phidias. In later times, the Macedonians added statues of Antigonus and Demetrius I Poliorketes, as well as the Macedonian king of Egypt, Ptolemy.

Continuing on, we can see the remains of two exedrae that were raised by the Argives. The one to the south (left) contained statues of the seven Epigoni, the successors of the mythical 'Seven Against Thebes', who avenged their predecessors by defeating and sacking Thebes. In the exedra to the north of the sacred way were the statues of ten mythical kings and queens of Argos (including Perseus, Alcmaeon and Heracles).

This series of votive monuments was completed by the offering of the Tarentines after their victory over the barbarian race of the Messapians in the 5th century BCE. The bronze statues presented horses and captive Messapian women.

The northern exedra of Argos.

The Treasury of the Sicyonians. The rear wall of the Syphnian Treasury is visible in the background.

Near the votive offering of the Tarentines is a treasury of the Sicyonians, ... (Pausanias: 10.11.1)

On the terrain of the Sanctuary of Apollo itself, 21 treasuries were erected. Just after the Monument of the Tarentines, we can see the remains of the Doric Treasury of the Sicyonians, built around 500 BCE by the residents of the city after overthrowing their tyrannical leader. It was a small building in the templum in antis style that stood on the site of two earlier (around 600–570 BCE) monopteral buildings, one of which probably contained a chariot exhibited by the tyrant Cleisthenes after his victory in the Pythian Games.

One of the most beautiful buildings of the sanctuary was the Syphnian Treasury, which stood opposite that of the Sicyonians. It was made of Parian marble and built around 525 BCE. Pausanias informs us that the construction of the treasury was funded using a tenth of the profits from the gold mine which was located on the island. It was a small (6.12 by 8.55 metres), Ionic building in the templum in antis style with caryatid statues used instead of columns in the portico. One of the richest combinations of archaic, Ionic, architectural sculpture can be admired on this treasury. The decoration of the gable presents the struggle between Apollo and Heracles for the Delphic Tripod, whilst on the continuous frieze are scenes depicting the abduction of the Leucippides by the Dioscuri, the judgement of Paris, the Gigantomachy and the gods watching over the Trojan War.

Continuing along the Sacred Way, we pass further treasuries, the vast majority of which were built in the 6th century BCE. These were constructed by the Liparians, the Beotians, the Cnidians and the citizens of Thebes (370 BCE), Thracian Potidaea, Megara, Klazomenai and Syracuse (412 BCE).

The Thebans have a treasury built from the spoils of war, and so have the Athenians. (Pausanias: 10.11.5)

Particular attention should be paid to the Doric Treasury of the Athenians, which was constructed in the classical templum in antis form. It was built around 500 BCE, was made entirely of Parian marble and measured 6.62 by 9.68 metres. Its relatively well-preserved 24 metopes present the deeds of Heracles and Theseus, as well as the Amazonomachy. Amongst the inscriptions found on the walls of the treasury are two fascinating hymns to Apollo with musical notation from the 2nd century BCE. The Athenian Treasury is thus far the only building within the sanctuary of Apollo to have been practically entirely reconstructed by French archaeologists (between 1903 and 1906).

Just after the Athenian Treasury are further rectangular remains in the form of a bouleuterion, as well as the Sybil Rock, where:

On it, say the Delphians, there stood and chanted the oracles a woman, by name Herophile and surnamed Sibyl. (Pausanias: 10.12.1).

The Treasury of the Athenians (on the left) and the Sibyl Rock (on the right).

The Stoa of the Athenians (in the foreground).

At the foot of the terrace upon which the Temple of Apollo was built, the Athenians built an eight-columned Ionic portico (stoa) to commemorate their victory over the Persians in 478 BCE. The portico was around thirty metres in length, four metres in breadth and contained the bows of ships which Xerxes had used to create a kind of pontoon bridge over the Hellespont Strait. Just to the west of the portico stood an over nine-metre high column with a sphinx, raised in honour of Apollo by the citizens of Naxos. Continuing on in the direction of the temple, we then pass the remains of the treasuries of the Corinthians (7th century BCE), the Kyrenians (4th century BCE) and the Acanthians (442 BCE).

The Pillar of Prusias.

Just in front of the entrance to the temple, an altar was erected in the 5th century BCE by the residents of the island of Chios. 8.58 metres high and 4.6 metres wide, it was made of black (the base) and white marble. Many differing types of monument stood around it including columns of Eumenes II (of Pergamon), Prusias II (of Bithynia), a magnificent Rhodian monument presenting Helios on his quadriga and the previously mentioned bronze column supporting a tripod, which commemorated the battle of Plataea.

In the fore-temple at Delphi are written maxims useful for the life of men, inscribed by those whom the Greeks say were sages. ... "Know thyself," and "Nothing in excess." (Pausanias: 10.24.1)

The most marvellous building of the sanctuary was without doubt the Temple of Apollo, which was built between 525 and 510 BCE with the financial backing of the Athenian Alcmaeonid family. It stood on the site of the previous temple, which dated to the 7th century BCE and burned down in 548 BCE. The Temple of Apollo was made of poros in the Doric peripteros style with measurements of 23.8 by 59.5 metres and arranged with six and fifteen-columned sides. Its interior included a pronaos, a cella and an opisthodomos. The cella was divided into two parts. The first included the altar of Poseidon and statues of two of the Moirai, whilst the part to the rear (the adyton) contained a gold statue of Apollo and also the place where the Pythia sat on a tripod speaking the words of the oracle.

The Temple of Apollo. View from the North-West.

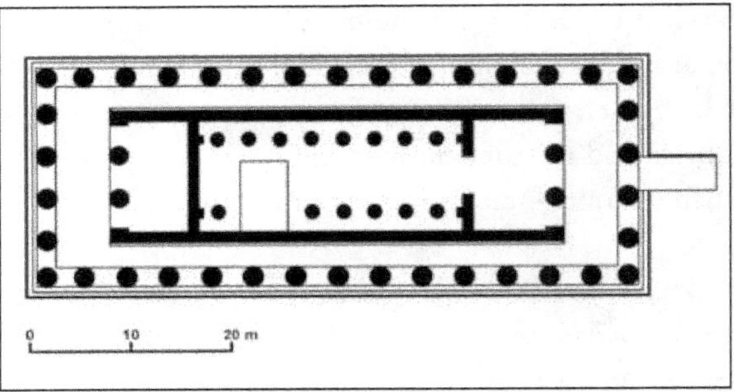

Plan of the Temple of Apollo.

The eastern temple gable was decorated with marble bas-reliefs presenting Apollo on his way to Delphi on his chariot, whilst a shield taken during the Persian wars was placed in lieu of a metope. In 373 BCE, the temple was destroyed by an earthquake, although it was quickly rebuilt. Only its foundations and several columns have survived to the present day.

Going around the right-hand side of the Temple of Apollo, we soon come to some remains lying to its north-west which are of the 'Ex-voto of Craterus'. It was built around 320 BCE by the son of Craterus, who was one of the generals of Alexander the Great. It was made of bronze by the famous sculptors Lysippos and Leochares and depicted Alexander during a lion hunt with General Craterus rushing to his aid.

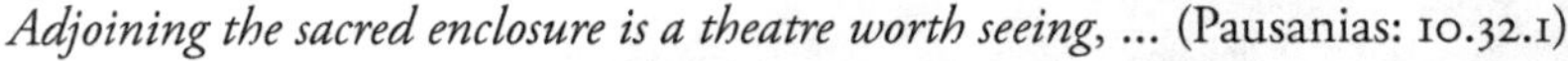
Adjoining the sacred enclosure is a theatre worth seeing, ... (Pausanias: 10.32.1)

The Ex-voto of Craterus.

The Theatre.

On the terrace which lies above the temple, there is a small theatre which once was used for both public gatherings and musical competitions. It was built in the 4th century BCE and then later rebuilt in 159 BCE thanks to the assistance of Eumenes II, the leader of Pergamon. The auditorium consisted of 35 rows of seating intended for approximately 5,000 spectators. It probably originally contained an orchestra with a diameter of 18.5 metres and, in a later period, it would have had a stage construction built onto it. In the Roman period, the auditorium side was decorated with a marble relief portraying the Labours of Heracles.

Beyond the Cassotis stands a building with paintings of Polygnotus. It was dedicated by the Cnidians, and is called by the Delphians Lesche [Place of Talk, Club Room], ... (Pausanias: 10.25.1)

Above the theatre, at the northern edge of the Sanctuary of Apollo, was the Cnidian Lesche. The building, which was constructed around 460 BCE in rectangular form with measurements of 9.7 by 18.7 metres, was decorated by splendid paintings by Polygnotus of Thasos.Pausanias dedicated a whole seven chapters (10.25–31) of his work to describing these paintings, which depicted scenes such as the Conquest of Troy, the Setting Sail of the Greeks and Odysseus' Descent into Hades.

The Stadium. View from the North-West.

The Delphian race-course is on the highest part of their city. (Pausanias: 10.32.1)

A stadium used during the Pythian Games was built in the 5th century BCE above the temenos of the Sanctuary of Apollo. An inscription from the time discovered by archaeologists prohibits the bringing of wine into the stadium and declares the fine to be five drachma. As was the case at Olympia, spectators would have originally watched the action while seated directly on the ground. It was only in the 2nd century CE, thanks to the funding of Herodes Atticus, that stone rows of seating intended for 7,000 spectators were built. Due to the shape of the land, the northern side held twelve rows of seats, whereas the south had only six. The stadium was 177.55 metres long and its breadth ranged from 25.25 to 28.5 metres. The start line (*aphesis*) was to the east and the finish line (*terma*) to the west.

The Castalian Spring, Gymnasium and Sanctuary of Athena

Ascending from the gymnasium along the way to the sanctuary you reach, on the right of the way, the water of Castalia, which is sweet to drink and pleasant to bathe in. (Pausanias: 10.8.9)

Pausanias approached Delphi from the east and so before he reached the Sanctuary of Apollo, he first visited the Sanctuary of Athena, the Gymnasium and the Castalian Spring. Today, however, most tourists tour the site in the reverse order.

Upon leaving the Sanctuary of Apollo and heading to the Athena complex (visible in the distance), we first pass the remains of the Castalian Spring (famous in ancient times) to our left. Those who paid a visit to the sanctuaries of Delphi were obliged to first ritually cleanse themselves in its waters. The place was given its magnificent architectonic framing in Hellenic and Roman times. A little higher are remains dating to the 6th to 5th centuries BCE.

Continuing onwards towards the Sanctuary of Athena, we come to the Gymnasium. This vast complex, which was finally completed in the 4th century BCE, contained a running track, a palaestra and baths. Due to the shape of the land, it was positioned on two terraces. On the upper one was a covered running track (xystos), which allowed for training to take place regardless of the weather. The track was approximately 184 metres long and its roof supported a Doric portico made of poros that was then replaced in Roman times by a marble Ionic portico.

The palaestra was built on the lower terrace and its central courtyard was surrounded by an Ionic portico. Adjacent rooms to the north and north-west of the courtyard were used by athletes for the embrocating of the body in olive oil and sand and also as a changing room. Another courtyard, which contained a round cistern in its centre to be used for bathing, also bordered

The Gymnasium (on the left) and the Sanctuary of Athena Pronaia (on the right).

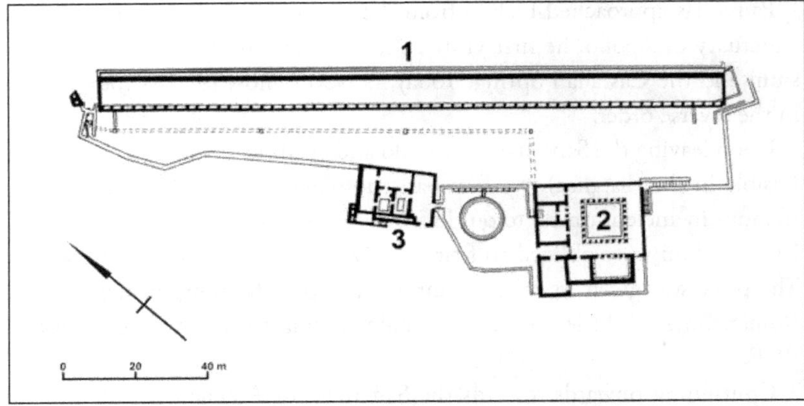

Plan of the Gymnasium: 1 – Xystos, 2 – Palaestra, 3 – Roman Baths.

the palaestra. Around 120 CE, new baths in typical Roman style were built within the Gymnasium.

When you enter the city you see temples in a row. The first of them was in ruins, and the one next to it had neither images nor statues. The third had statues of a few Roman emperors; the fourth is called the temple of Athena Forethought. (Pausanias: 10.8.6)

Delphi contained one more temple complex, the Sanctuary of Athena of Forethought. Over the course of archaeological research, two temples of Athena have been discovered here.

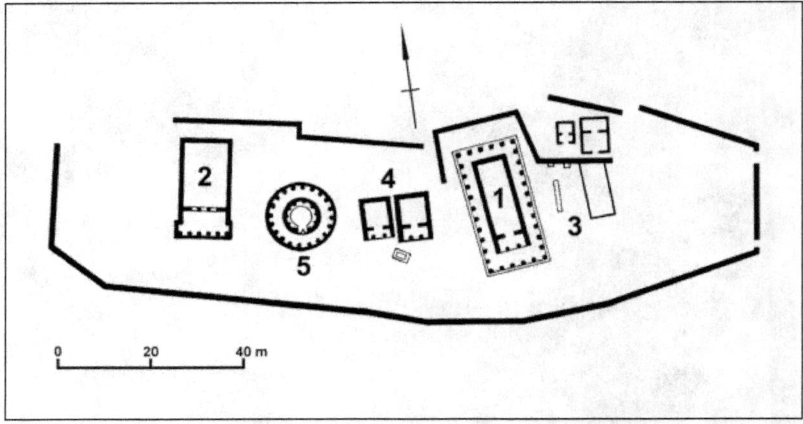

Plan of the Sanctuary of Athena Pronaia: 1 – First Temple of Athena, 2 – Second Temple of Athena, 3 – Altars, 4 – Treasuries, 5 – Tholos.

The first, a Doric temple of the goddess built around 650 BCE, was destroyed by a falling boulder of rock. It was then reconstructed towards the end of the 6th century BCE by making use of the earlier material. This new temple was also of the Doric peripteros style with measurements of 13 by 28 metres and six and twelve columned sides. Its interior simply consisted of a pronaos and an extended cella. Further restoration work was carried out on the temple after the earthquake of 373 BCE. In the 4th century BCE, a second temple was built in honour of the goddess. It was of the Doric prostylos type with six columns in its façade and was a rectangular construction with measurements of 11.55 by 22.6 metres. Two Ionic half columns were placed at the entrance between the pronaos and the cella.

The Athena complex also contained altars (dedicated to Athena, Hygieia and Eileithyia amongst others) and two treasuries, including one of Massalia (present day Marseille in France).

However, the most interesting building of this area is the Tholos, which was built at the beginning of the 4th century BCE by the architect, Theodorus. Although it is one of the most marvellous constructions of Delphi, researchers today still do not know what function it performed. It was a

The Tholos in the Sanctuary of Athena Pronaia.

round building of Parian marble with a diameter of 13.5 metres surrounded by a peristasis made up of twenty Doric columns. The half columns of the interior of the cella were, however, Corinthian. The building was decorated by two Doric friezes depicting scenes from the Amazonomachy and the Centauromachy. It is interesting to note that Pausanias made no mention at all of the Tholos, which suggests the possibility that it was already a ruin in his times.

PRACTICAL INFORMATION:

Delphi is both one of the most important and most interesting archaeological sites of Greece. An additional attraction is its extremely picturesque location in Phocis (central Greece) on the southern slope of Mount Parnassus. It should therefore be of little surprise that hordes of tourists flock here throughout the year. In order to avoid this mass of humanity, it is advisable to arrive when the gates open in the early morning.

Zeus (Poseidon?) of Artemision.

Delphi can be reached by car from Athens (180km) in around two to three hours, travelling through Thebes and Livadeia. The stretch of road between Livadeia and Delphi is blessed with wonderful scenery, especially in the area close to the mountain spa town of Arachova.

Delphi can also be reached from Patras in the Peloponnese by first crossing the Rio-Antirrio Bridge and then turning east towards Itea (Road 48) with the Corinthian Gulf on your right. This journey takes around two hours and is considerably more interesting than taking the road from Athens, largely due to the fact that it runs along the coastline of the Corinthian Gulf between Naupactus and Itea.

Delphi can be visited as a day trip from Athens or Patras, but it is much more advisable to stay for at least two days and to find accommodation in one of the small hotels which can be found in the modern village of Delphi, particularly those which boast extensive views of the Corinthian Gulf.

As indicated above, it is best to come early to the site to avoid the crowds. For the same reason, it is also advisable to first visit the two sanctuaries and then the local archaeological museum at the end.

The ancient architectural monuments which cannot be missed at Delphi are as follows, starting from the side of the entrance to the Sanctuary of Apollo:

- *The Treasury of the Athenians*
- *The Temple of Apollo*
- *The Theatre*
- *The Stadium*
- *The Tholos (found within the sacred precinct of Athena and one of the most photographed monuments in Greece).*

Relief decoration of the Syphnian Treasury.

The archaeological museum of Delphi is one of the most important of its kind in Greece. It contains a wonderful collection of ancient art, which includes objects found at Delphi by French archaeologists. Amongst these, the bronze statue of the 'Charioteer of Delphi', the marble statues of Kleobis and Biton, the marble omphalos (the mythical navel of the world) and the relief decoration of the Athenian and Syphnian treasuries are worthy of special attention.

The Site and the Museum:

Open: *Monday-Sunday: 8 a.m. – 7 p.m.*

Tickets: *Full – 6 Euros; Reduced – 3 Euros*

Special ticket package valid for the site and the museum: Full – 9 Euros, Reduced – 5 Euros

Free admission days: *6 March, 18 April, 18 May, 5 June, 27 September, 28 October, the last weekend of September, every first Sunday from November 1st to March 31st*

Site closed: *1 January, 25 March, Easter Sunday, 1 May, 25–26 December*

It should be remembered that many people (from member states of the European Union) are entitled to free entry to the archaeological sites of Greece. This includes those over 65 or under 18, students and academic instructors.

It is always worth checking at the entrance about the possibility of a discount to the ticket price. A website prepared by the Greek Ministry of Tourism is also of assistance in this matter: http://odysseus.culture.gr/index_en.html

The Temple of Apollo. View from the South-East.

CORINTH

Ancient Corinth lies within the north-eastern Peloponnese between the Corinthian and Saronic Gulfs. Acrocorinth, a mighty rock elevation (575 metres above sea level), towers over the city, dominating the Isthmus of Corinth and at the same time the passage between central Greece and the Peloponnese. Corinth possessed a port on both sides of the isthmus in Lechaeum (on the Corinthian Gulf) and Kenchreai (on the Saronic Gulf), which allowed it to control sea traffic. This was especially true after the construction of the 'Diolkos' towards the end of the 6th century BCE, a paved track way which permitted the hauling of ships from one gulf to the other.

The things worthy of mention in the city [Corinth – W.M.] include the extant remains of antiquity, but the greater number of them belong to the period of its second ascendancy. (Pausanias: 2.2.6)

Corinth was one of the most important centres in the development of Greek culture and art. Legend has it that the city was originally called Ephyra after the oceanid of the same name, who is said to have been its first inhabitant. The later name comes from the mythical founder of the city, Corinthus, whom the residents of Corinth believed to be the son of Zeus himself. According to Pausanias, however, no other Hellenic Greeks believed this.

The earliest traces of inhabitation come from small settlements on nearby elevations (including the site of Korakou) dating to the Late Neolithic period (6000–3100 BCE) and the Early Bronze Age (3100–2000 BCE). During the times of the Mycenaean civilisation (1600–1200 BCE), many small settlements sprang up around Corinth, but none of these was an important administrative centre, as has been confirmed by archaeological research. The leader of Mycenae therefore probably had control of Corinth in the Late Bronze Age. However, as certain researchers have stated, it is also possible that the site of ancient Corinth did possess an important Mycenaean administrative centre that was subsequently completely destroyed.

The beginnings of ancient Corinth date back to the 10th century BCE. In the 8th century BCE, the residents of Corinth, using their advantageous geographical position, began to play a leading role in Greek trade and the colonisation of the West. The city began to rapidly expand, largely thanks to it being involved in a great deal of trade, but also because of its overseas colonies, which included Syracuse (Sicily) and Korkyra (Corfu), the latter of which was founded around 734 BCE. The best artists and artisans came to Corinth at this time. Their work, which included decorative pottery and bronze objects, was admired and

The Temple of Apollo.

highly valued across antiquity. The city was also surrounded by an impressive fortification system of dried brick, which encompassed the centre, the port of Lechaeum and stretched as far as Acrocorinth.

The marble head of Julius Caesar at Corinth Archaeological Museum.

During the Peloponnesian Wars (459–446 then 431–404 BCE), the inhabitants of Corinth fought on the side of the Spartans. Later, however, they fought with the armies of Thebes, Argos and Athens against their former allies in the Corinthian War (395–387 BCE), in order to weaken the dominant position of the Spartans within the Peloponnese. From 338 to 196 BCE, Corinth was subjugated by the Macedonians, albeit with a few brief interruptions to their rule. Halfway through the 2nd century BCE, the citizens of Corinth persuaded the remaining members of the Achaean League to go to war with the Romans (146 BCE). As a result, the Roman army of Consul Lucius Mummius plundered and totally destroyed the city, slaying or putting into slavery all of its residents. It was only 100 years later, in 44 BCE, that Julius Caesar ordered Corinth to be rebuilt as a Roman colony, intended primarily for freedmen and war veterans. Soon afterwards, in 27 BCE, Corinth became the administrative capital of the Roman province of Achaea and an important centre of the emperor cult. During the rule of Emperor Claudius, the Holy Apostle Paul founded one of the first Christian communities here.

In the 2nd century CE, Corinth experienced a boom in construction as many buildings of public use were rebuilt, partly thanks to the financial backing of Herodes Atticus. In 396 CE, the city was taken by the army of Alaric. Following this invasion, new fortifications were constructed in the 5th century CE, which encompassed only around a third of the previously defended area. Thereafter, Corinth continued to function until the 7th or 8th century CE, when it was abandoned.

Archaeological research on the area of ancient Corinth began towards the end of the 19th century. It was first led by the famous German researcher of Greek antiquity, Wilhelm Dörpfeld. From 1896 up until the present day, his work has been continued by researchers affiliated with the American School of Classical Studies in Athens.

The Site

A visit to ancient Corinth should begin at the local archaeological museum, where it is possible to view a small collection of objects discovered by American researchers during their excavations presented in chronological order. After seeing the museum, we can then head in the direction of Temple Hill where the partly preserved colonnade (*peristasis*) of the Temple of Apollo can already be seen from afar.

As you go along another road from the market-place, which leads to Sicyon, you can see on the right of the road a temple and bronze image of Apollo, and a little farther on a well called the Well of Glauce. (Pausanias: 2.3.6)

Protocorinthian oinochoe at Corinth Archaeological Museum.

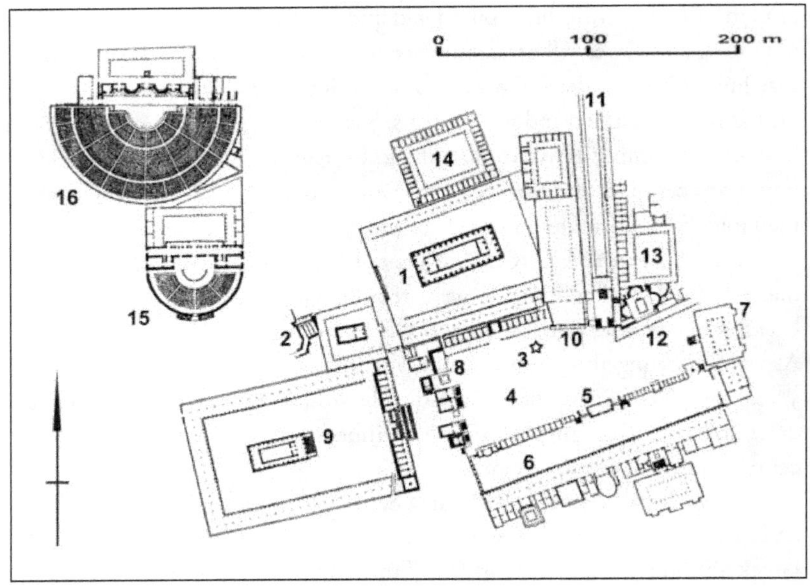

Plan of ancient Corinth: 1 – Temple of Apollo, 2 – Fountain of Glauke, 3 – Sacred Spring, 4 – Forum, 5 – Rostra, 6 – South Stoa, 7 – Basilica, 8 – Monument of Babbius, 9 – Temple of Octavia, 10 – Captives Façade, 11 – Lechaeum Road, 12 – Fountain of Peirene, 13 – Sacred Precinct of Apollo, 14 – North Market, 15 – Odeon, 16 – Theatre (after Wiliams, Zervos, 1991, Fig. 4).

The most important building from the period preceding the Roman destruction of the city was the Doric Temple of Apollo, which stands on Temple Hill. The first temple was built here around 680–670 BCE and was a stone building without a peristasis. It was covered by a roof of terracotta tiles, the earliest known example of such roofing in Greece. Around halfway through the 6th century BCE, the temple was consumed by a fire and a new construction replaced it, the remains of which we can admire today. The new temple was a Doric peripteros with six by fifteen columns. On some of these, traces of molding have been preserved, a typical decorative element of the Archaic period.

The stylobate measured 21.49 by 53.82 metres, but the precise layout out of the interior is uncertain, since Roman colonists later altered it. An example of this was their removal of the interior columns, which they then used in the south-west portico of the Forum. We can, however, be sure that the interior of the temple in pre-Roman times consisted of three parts. These were a cella, fronted by a pronaos to the east and backed by an opisthodomos to the west.

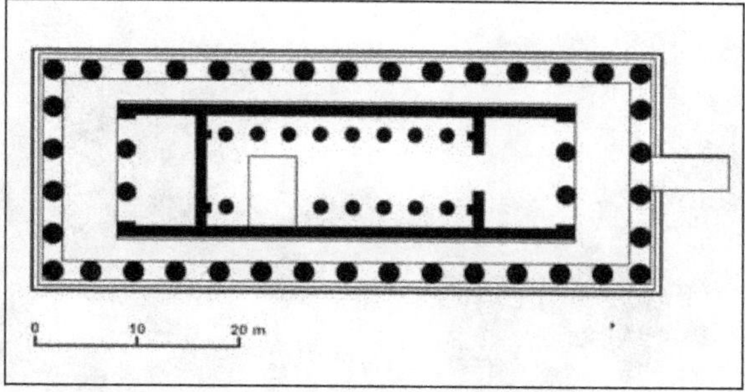

Plan of the Temple of Apollo.

The cella was divided into two rooms by a massive wall. Some researchers now believe that the western room could have been entered via the opisthodomos, whilst others contend that the dividing wall of the cella contained a door and that the rear section (to the west) was an adyton (the holiest place of the temple that only priests could enter). Both parts of the cella were further divided by two rows of columns into a main nave and two aisles. Unfortunately, none of the sculptural decoration of the Temple of Apollo has survived to our times.

From the Archaic period onwards, Temple Hill was accessed via monumental steps found on its south-eastern side. In the Roman period, however,

The Temple of Apollo. Remains of the interior.

The Fountain of Glauke. View from the East.

these were moved to the western side. This was done as a result of the architectural reconstruction of the entire hill, which included the erection of two new porticos on the northern and southern sides.

Other constructions from pre-Roman times include the remains of the Fountain of Glauke (6th century BCE), rooms built around the Sacred Spring next to which the oracle performed (6th century BCE), the south portico of the Forum (4th century BCE) and the Theatre (end of the 5th century BCE). However, these were all later rebuilt by the Romans.

The remains of the Fountain of Glauke are currently visible between Temple Hill and the museum building. The fountain consisted of a series of rock-cut tanks, into which water was transported via pipes from a spring which lay somewhere to the south of Corinth. Pausanias explained that the name of the complex came from Glauke, the daughter of the king of Corinth, Kreon. Glauke is supposed to have thrown herself into the water here after being cruelly poisoned by Medea. In revenge for this deed, the inhabitants of Corinth stoned Medea's sons, Mermerus and Pheres, to death.

The beginnings of the Fountain of Glauke have traditionally been dated to the 6th century BCE, although some researchers now believe that it was constructed in the Hellenistic period. After its destruction in 146 BCE, it was rebuilt by Roman colonists sent by Caesar. The large cube of rock visible today is what remains of a natural elevation first used as a quarry. The interior contained the abovementioned four water tanks, which were fronted

The Forum. View from the North-East.

by rock-cut pools to which steps led. The construction was completed by a wonderful, decorative façade that has not survived to our times.

After visiting Temple Hill, we turn to the south in the direction of the Roman Forum, once the centre of the city and now visible to the left of the museum building.

The remains of ancient Corinth that we can now admire come mostly from Roman times. This is because Roman architects constructed an entirely

West Side of the Forum.

new city of Corinth from the rubble of the previous one (around the beginning of the Common Era), which they built along Roman lines.

On the market-place, where most of the sanctuaries are, ... (Pausanias: 2.2.6)

The western part of the Roman Forum contained the 'western shops'. These were fronted by a magnificent Corinthian colonnade, which in turn was fronted by a vast terrace with a series of small temples. Each of these possessed a rectangular cella fronted by a vestibule with four columns in its façade. Only the platforms have survived to our times, meaning that their dating and the identification of the gods to whom they were dedicated remains hypothetical, despite the clues which Pausanias offers us. In any case, the temple situated to the north of the terrace (which has been marked 'D') was probably dedicated to the goddess, Tyche (Fortuna). The two Corinthian temples labelled 'J' and 'H' were constructed during the reign of Emperor Commodus, as is attested by Latin inscriptions on the façades (in both cases the name, Commodus, was later removed). These were most probably dedicated to Poseidon and Heracles respectively. To the south of them, temple 'G' was dedicated to Apollo of Claros (a city in Asia Minor), whilst the adjacent temple 'F' honoured the goddess, Venus Genetrix ('Mother'), and was built at the beginning of the 1st century CE.

In the northern section of the terrace, the remains of the Monument of Babbius (probably a wealthy freedman) can be seen. It was constructed in the 1st century CE and is supposed to have been an eight-columned Corinthian monopteros, topped by a conical roof and positioned on a high platform.

Above the market-place is a temple of Octavia the sister of Augustus, who was emperor of the Romans after Caesar, the founder of the modern Corinth. (Pausanias: 2.3.1)

Between the two rows of western shops mentioned above (six per row) was the monumental entrance to a vast courtyard, which was surrounded on three sides by porticos and in the centre of which stood a temple (marked 'E' by archaeologists), one of the most marvellous buildings of Corinth. It was constructed at the beginning of the 1st century CE in the Doric style with six columns in its façade. Towards the end of the 1st century CE, however, it was completely rebuilt. The new construction was now in the Corinthian style and was placed on a high platform. It was surrounded by a peristasis with six columns on its shorter sides and twelve on the longer ones. The interior of the temple contained an extended rectangular cella fronted by a short

The Temple of Octavia.

pronaos, with two columns positioned between the antae. Temple 'E' was probably dedicated to Jupiter Capitolinus or, as Pausanias suggests, Octavia, the sister of Emperor Augustus.

The centre of Roman Corinth was the Forum (agora), which was paved with marble slabs and measured 65 by 165 metres. Below the Roman Forum, archaeologists have discovered the remains of two stadiums, one dating to the Archaic and one to the Hellenistic period. The starting blocks (*apheteria* in Greek) of both were found somewhat to the west of the later Julian Basilica. Unfortunately, the precise length of the stadiums is unknown, although we do know that the stadium's positioning was slightly different in the two cases.

The Roman Forum was divided into upper (to the south) and lower (to the north) sections by the 'central shops' that ran through its centre. These premises were built from 25 to 50 CE and were probably used by the bankers whose work contributed to the fame of Corinth in Roman times. The eastern section comprised fifteen rooms, of which the largest were in the centre and probably used by a cult. The western contained fourteen further shops and an additional small structure, currently believed to have been a cult place of Dionysus or Hermes.

Between the rows of shops was a high podium called the Rostra, built around halfway through the 1st century CE. It had the appearance of an open

The Rostra in the middle of the Forum. Acrocorinth is in the background.

propylon and stood on a rectangular platform of 7.2 by 15.6 metres that was about three metres high. Steps connecting the upper and lower sections of the forum ran down its sides. In the Middle Ages, the Rostra was identified as the platform from which Proconsul Junius Gallaicus refused to investigate the case of the Corinthian Jews against the Christian, Paul (around 52 CE).

The South Stoa.

A stoa on two levels was built in the southern part of the Forum, unsurprisingly now known as the South Stoa. The beginnings of this huge construction (measuring 25.15 by 164.38 metres) date to the end of the 4th century BCE and it was initially a double colonnade (71 Doric outer columns and 34 Ionic inner columns) containing a row of 33 shops, each with two rooms. Some of these were used as canteens.

When the Romans reconstructed the portico, many of its former rooms were transformed into complexes of multifarious orchestration and purpose. The Bouleuterion, an elliptical building which hosted the city council, was built more or less in the centre of the portico. Even today, parts of its benches (where officials would have sat) can be discerned. Just next to the Bouleuterion, a paved way leading to the port of Kenchreai began. The following buildings were located a little further to the east: a small, but richly decorated nymphaeum, the monumental entrance to the southern basilica and a rectangular room, next to which a monument dedicated to Gaius Cerealis, the Procurator of the province of Achaea during the rule of Emperor Hadrian, stood. This room may even have been his office. Another room lying further to the east was probably used by officials responsible for the organisation of the Isthmian Games, since its floor mosaic (from around 50–100 CE) depicts a winning competitor standing next to the seated Fortuna.

In the Roman period, a building fronted by a small Ionic portico dating to 25–50 CE stood in the south-east corner of the Forum. Previously, the city archive or a library would have been situated here (second half of the 1st century BCE).

On the eastern side of the Forum are the remains of a large basilica built during the reign of Emperor Augustus. It was a two-storey building made of local limestone, richly decorated with marble lining and statues, including those of Augustus and Nero. Legal cases were probably heard here and it is likely it was also a centre of the emperor cult.

In the northern part of the Forum, the remains of the Sacred Spring (dating to the beginning of the 6th century BCE) can be found, It was not, however, a typical water spring, but rather a small sanctuary. It consisted of a modest building constructed over the 'spring' and an open courtyard, within which an altar made of earth (*eschara*) was situated. The courtyard was surrounded by a low triglyph-metope wall. An inscription found during archaeological research informs us that the area around the spring was sacred: *Sacrosanct (land). None may enter. Fine: eight (oboloi).* Furthermore, archaeologists have come across a small tunnel in this area which connected the sanctuary to a nearby building with an apse (perhaps a temple).

Remains of the Sacred Spring (behind the triglyph-metope wall) in the Forum.

According to one theory, this could have been used as a room for a hidden priest (perhaps an oracle), who divined the will of the gods under the floor of the temple.

The 'north-western shops', which date to the beginning of the 2nd century CE and were fronted by a colonnade, were located in the northern part of the Forum just next to the remains of the Sacred Spring. A long two-storey portico (the north-west stoa) ran between them and the temenos of the Temple of Apollo. This was built during the reign of Emperor Augustus and had measurements of approximately 9 by 101 metres. The portico contained 47 Doric outer columns and twenty Ionic inner columns.

The remains of another small, two-storey portico known as the Captives Façade can also be seen in the northern part of the Forum, to the east of the north-western shops. The name of the portico derives from the decoration of its upper floor, which was once adorned with statues of barbarians and personifications of lands of the East (preserved examples of which are now found within the museum). Despite the fact that many of its architectonic elements come from the times of Emperor Augustus, researchers consider that it should be dated to the years 160–170 BCE or the beginning of the 3rd century CE. In the first instance, it would commemorate the victory over the Parthian armies won by Emperor Lucius Verus, whilst in the second case it would be those won by Emperor Septimius Severus.

After visiting the Forum, we now turn to the north, in the direction of the preserved remains of the marvellous Lechaeum Road.

On leaving the market-place along the road to Lechaeum you come to a gateway, on which are two gilded chariots, … (Pausanias: 2.3.2)

A monumental, triple-arched gateway once stood just next to the Captives Façade. It was constructed at the beginning of the 1st century CE and was decorated with two gilded chariots carrying Helios and his son, Phaethon. Behind it, the Lechaeum Road began its route to the port. Unfortunately, only the remains of the gate's foundations have survived to our times.

The wonderful Lechaeum Road has fared much better, however. It was the main north to south artery of the city (*cardo maximus* in Latin) and it began below a set of monumental steps leading from the abovementioned triple-arched gate. The road was built at the beginning of the 1st century CE and it was then paved with limestone slabs during the rule of Emperor Vespasian (69–79 CE). Porticos which ran along the pavement (raised one level) on both sides were also constructed at this time.

The Lechaeum Road.

The Fountain of Peirene.

The spring [Peirene] is ornamented with white marble, and there have been made chambers like caves, out of which the water flows into an open-air well. (Pausanias: 2.3.3)

Just after the Forum, to the east (right) of the Lechaeum Road, the remains of the Fountain of Peirene (of great renown in antiquity) can be found. According to Pausanias, it was here that the nymph, Peirene, turned into a spring whilst weeping because of the untimely death of her son, Cenchrias, who had been accidentally shot by Artemis.

Archaeological research has shown that the first work involving water collection was undertaken here as early as the Geometric period. By the 2nd century BCE, six chambers allowing access to three deep, rock-cut water tanks had been created. These were replenished by underground water-pipes of around 500 metres in length. The wonderful architectonic framing of the complex, the remains of which we can still admire today, was created during the rule of Emperor Augustus and then made more elaborate during the period of major reconstruction towards the end of the 2nd century CE.

The Fountain of Peirene was undoubtedly one of the most beautiful sights of ancient Corinth. The complex consisted of a small peristyle containing a rectangular tank that was topped up with water by channels running under

The north wall of the Fountain of Peirene.

the floor of the courtyard. Richly ornamented exedrae were constructed on three of the sides of the courtyard, whilst the fourth boasted a richly decorated wall containing six chambers with curved ceilings. Steps on the northern side of the complex led down to underground tanks where water was collected. The whole site was laid with splendid white marble, which was later admired by Pausanias, as well as many others.

Moreover near Peirene are an image and a sacred enclosure of Apollo; ... (Pausanias: 2.3.3)

Directly to the north of the Fountain of Peirene and still further to the right of the Lechaeum Road is a complex dated by archaeologists to the end of the 1st century CE. It was described by Pausanias as a sacred precinct and was decorated with statues of Apollo and paintings depicting Odysseus killing the suitors of Penelope. It consisted of a rectangular courtyard (with measurements of 23 by 32 metres) surrounded by Ionic colonnades and an apse to the south. During archaeological investigation here, part of its architectonic decoration (which would once have been on the colonnade) was discovered. This consisted of the relief of a ship on one side and an inscription naming the donor who financed the complex on the other (a member of the Emilius family). The complex was probably built on the site of an earlier fish market (*macellum* in Latin), which would have existed during the rule

The relief of a ship from the sacred precinct of Apollo.

of Emperor Augustus. This is attested by Latin inscriptions discovered by archaeologists in its vicinity.

To the north of the sacred precinct of Apollo are the remains of the Eurycles Baths (mentioned by Pausanias), which were constructed in the 1st century CE and then rebuilt in the 2nd century CE. On the other side of the Lechaeum Road, the remains of a great basilica (with measurements of around 25 by 70 metres) are situated, which archaeologists date to the end of the 1st century BCE. Its main entrance was on the side of the Forum and it could be reached through a small courtyard behind the Captives Façade.

The remains of the North Market, probably dating to the 1st century CE, extend to the north of the basilica and the temenos of the Temple of Apollo. It was a small columned courtyard surrounded by forty rooms that were used as either shops or offices.

Above this well [Glauke] has been built what is called the Odeum (Music Hall), ... (Pausanias: 2.3.6)

The Odeon and the Theatre were located to the north-west of the centre of ancient Corinth. They now lie outside the confines of the tourist site, just next to the parking lot for buses. The remains of the Odeon are directly to the west of the car park, whilst the place where the Theatre once stood is a bit further north.

The Odeon.

The Corinthian Odeon was a kind of covered concert hall intended for around 3,000 spectators. It was built in the 1st century CE and then rebuilt around halfway through the 2nd century CE thanks to funds provided by Herodes Atticus. During its reconstruction, new elements were added, including an open courtyard connecting the Odeon to the Theatre, whilst the slabs fronting its façade were exchanged for marble ones.

The Theatre. The Gulf of Corinth is in the background.

At the beginning of the 3rd century CE, the Corinthian Odeon was consumed by a fire. During its reconstruction, it was adapted in order to host gladiator fights and wild animal hunts (*venatio* in Latin). This was done by removing the stage and introducing a wall two metres in height in front of the lowest row of seating. It continued in this form until the end of the 4th century CE, when it was destroyed and abandoned for the final time.

Somewhat to the north of the Odeon, the Theatre (currently off limits to tourists) was constructed towards the end of the 5th century BCE in typical Greek style, by making use of a natural slope. In the Hellenistic period, a stage building was added (*skene* in Greek), as well as a new orchestra. The Theatre was then rebuilt by Roman colonists, probably at the beginning of the 1st century CE. During the rule of Emperor Hadrian, a new, marble stage building was constructed. Each of its three floors were richly adorned with friezes and reliefs (depicting scenes including the Gigantomachy, the Amazonomachy and the deeds of Hercules), parts of which can now be viewed in the courtyard of the museum.

The fortifications of Acrocorinth.

At the beginning of the 3rd century CE, the orchestra was converted into an arena intended for gladiator fights and the hunting of wild animals. Later, towards the end of the 3rd century CE, it was again altered, this time becoming an artificial lake designed to host sea battles (*naumachia* in Greek).

Acrocorinth

The Acrocorinthus is a mountain peak above the city, … (Pausanias: 2.4.6)

The mighty rock formation towering over Corinth from the south is called Acrocorinth. If you have a car, it is possible to drive up it on an easy, tarmac road. The road is several kilometres long and can also be covered on foot. If you choose the latter option, you will be able to enjoy beautiful views to the north and west.

Archaeologists have discovered traces of a settlement from the times of the Mycenaean civilisation at the peak of Acrocorinth. However, the impressive fortifications which are now visible on the elevation were mainly constructed in medieval times. These were built directly on top of the existing foundations of ancient walls.

The Greek and Macedonian fortifications were destroyed at the end of the 1st century BCE by the Roman legionaries of General Mummius. The only part to survive was the large tower which now stands to the right of the second medieval gate. It still possesses its original front of over eleven metres in height and it was once flanked by a gate located to the west of the elevation, to which there is a relatively gentle ascent.

The tower, which is dated to the 4th century BCE, is seen by archaeologists as evidence of the strengthening of the fortifications between 335 and 243 BCE, the period during which a Macedonian garrison occupied Acrocorinth. Despite the improved defences, the leader of the Achaean League, Aratos, was able to take the fortress with a group of 400 soldiers in 243 BCE in a surprise night attack.

On the summit of the Acrocorinthus is a temple of Aphrodite. (Pausanias: 2.5.1)

Acrocorinth. The place where the Temple of Aphrodite once stood. The Corinthian Isthmus is in the background.

On the peak itself, the remains of a stone building that researchers believe to have been a small temple of Aphrodite are situated. According to Pausanias, Helios gave Acrocorinth to the goddess of love (after he had been given it himself by Briareus) and this was why her temple was built in its centre. In the temple, the construction of which dates to the 5th century BCE, sacred prostitution was practised on a massive scale.

Strabo (8.6.20) wrote this of the temple:

And the temple of Aphrodite was so rich that it owned more than a thousand temple slaves, courtesans, whom both men and women had dedicated to the goddess. And therefore it was also on account of these women that the city was crowded with people and grew rich; for instance, the ship captains freely squandered their money, and hence the proverb, "Not for every man is the voyage to Corinth."

Close to the Sanctuary of Aphrodite lies a spring which was struck as a gift for King Sisyphus from the god, Asopus. This was done in exchange for information on the whereabouts of the god's daughter, Aegina, who had been kidnapped by Zeus. For this deed, Sisyphus was given a terribly cruel punishment in Hades, where he was forced to endlessly push a massive boulder to the top of a steep hill from whence it always rolled back down.

Another name of the spring is the Upper Peirene Spring. According to one myth, it was here that the winged horse, Pegasus, was captured by the hero, Bellerophon, whilst drinking from its waters.

PRACTICAL INFORMATION:

The archaeological site of Corinth is located in the modern day village of Archaia Korinthos in the north-eastern Peloponnese, between the Corinthian Gulf and the Saronic Gulf. The mighty Acrocorinth elevation towers over both the site and the Isthmus of Corinth, the passage between central Greece and the Peloponnese.

Corinth was one of the most important centres in the development of Greek art and culture and is therefore naturally one of the prime destinations for those interested in ancient Greek civilisation.

Ancient Corinth can be visited as a day trip from either Athens or Nafplio. If travelling from the capital, the car journey (85km) should take around an hour and from Nafplio (50km) it should take about the same amount of time. Trains and buses can also be taken (both from Athens and Nafplio) to the modern day city of Corinth, from whence a further eight kilometres must be covered on foot, by taxi or by local bus.

A little difficulty is posed by the last stretch of road before the site (above all due to vague signposting), but wherever you park the car within the village of Archaia Korinthos, the site should be no further than ten minutes distant.

It is advisable to begin your visit to ancient Corinth at the local archaeological museum, where you can view a small, chronologically ordered collection of objects found by American researchers over the course of their excavations. After leaving the museum, you should then make for 'Temple Hill', as is suggested in our guide. The must-sees are the Temple of Apollo, the Temple of Octavia, the Forum, the Fountain of Peirene and the Lechaeum Road. After your walk around ancient Corinth, it is then possible to cast a glance in the direction of the Odeon and the Theatre (located near to the car park), which are, unfortunately, currently off limits to tourists.

For those still with energy to burn, a trip to the summit of Acrocorinth beckons. By car, it is only a ten minute drive up a comfortable asphalt road, but it can also be reached by covering the several kilometres the road runs on foot. By taking the latter option, you will be able to enjoy beautiful views to the north and west of Acrocorinth. However, around three hours will be required for such an undertaking.

A walk around the fortress at the summit takes around one to one-and-a-half hours. You should remember to take a suitable amount of water and provisions with you, as it will not be possible to replenish your supplies at all times.

If you have a car, a trip to Corinth can easily be combined with a visit to the Sanctuary of Zeus at Nemea, which is located around 25 kilometres to the south-west of Corinth.

Corinth Archaeological Site and Museum:
Open: *1 April – 31 October: Monday-Sunday: 8 a.m. – 8 p.m.*
1 November – 31 March: Monday-Sunday: 8 a.m. – 3 p.m.
Tickets for both the Museum and the Archaeological Site: Full – 6 Euros; Reduced – 3 Euros
Free admission days: *6 March, 18 April, 18 May, 5 June, 28 October, last weekend of September, 1st Sunday of each month from 1 November until 31 March*
Site closed: *1 January, 25 March, Easter Sunday, 1 May, 25–26 December*

Acrocorinth:
Open: *Monday-Sunday: 8 a.m. – 3 p.m.*
Tickets: *Full – 2 Euros; Reduced – 1 Euro*
Free admission days: *27 September, Sundays in the period between 1 November and 31 March*

It should be remembered that many people (from member states of the European Union) are entitled to free entry to the archaeological sites of Greece. This includes those over 65 or under 18, students and academic instructors.

It is always worth checking at the entrance about the possibility of a discount to the ticket price. A website prepared by the Greek Ministry of Tourism is also of assistance in this matter: http://odysseus.culture.gr/index_en.html

The Lion Gate.

MYCENAE

Ascending to Tretus, and again going along the road to Argos, you see on the left the ruins of Mycenae. (Pausanias: 2.15.4)

Continuing his journey south towards the city of Argos, Pausanias visited the once mighty Mycenae, which in his times was already in ruin.

Mycenae lies on a small rock elevation in the north-western part of Argolis, in the vicinity of an old trade route leading from Corinth to Argos. It was control over this route (the main road connecting the Peloponnese and Attica with the more northerly Boeotia and Thessaly), as well as its fertile surrounding land, that was the source of the riches and power of the leaders of the city.

According to a legend related by Pausanias, Mycenae was founded by Perseus, the son of Zeus and Danae. The aglet (*mykes* in Greek) is supposed to have fallen from the sheath of his sword in this place, which he believed augured well for the founding of a city. In later years, Mycenae became the base of the mighty Agamemnon, who led the Greek army to Troy. After his victorious return, however, he was murdered along with his friends by his wife, Clytemnestra, and her lover, Aegisthus. The killers received their just desserts shortly afterwards, however, as they were put to death by Orestes, the son of Agamemnon and the future ruler of nearly the whole Peloponnese.

People were living in the surroundings of Mycenae as early as the Neolithic period (as proved by numerous archaeological studies), but the importance of the city only began to increase in the Middle Bronze Age. The earliest stone architectural remains discovered by archaeologists date to this time, as well as the more important necropolis found at the foot of the later citadel. The dead also started to be buried in one of the famous Mycenaean grave circles in this period.

In the past, researchers were largely convinced that these were the graves of a foreign royal dynasty, whose representatives had travelled from the north, subjugated the local people and built a fortress in Mycenae. Nevertheless, it was later noticed that the style of burial mimicked earlier customs and traditions in the area, with the only difference being the fact that the graves were considerably more richly furnished. The majority of researchers currently believe that the ruler of Mycenae was from a local dynasty and are therefore trying to answer a series of fundamental questions: How did the Mycenaeans become so rich? Did they gain their wealth by robbing and plundering the islands of the Aegean Sea (e.g. the affluent city of Phylakopi on the island of Milos) and the cities and palaces of Crete? Did they serve as mercenaries in Egypt? Although the above theories all seem plausible, the most likely answer is that the city's great increase in wealth should be attributed to trade. In the period under discussion, there were numerous trade routes running from the Near East, Egypt and Crete to Greece and Northern Europe. It would have been possible to attain great wealth in a very short period of time by assuming control and profiting from them.

From around 1500 BCE, the Mycenaean leaders started to be buried in increasingly elaborate tombs. These included the great Tholos Tombs, at least nine of which were constructed around Mycenae. Unfortunately, they were all looted in antiquity, but there is not the slightest doubt amongst researchers that they were used to inter the Mycenaean kings (including the mythical Agamemnon) with their wondrous riches.

The mighty fortifications of Mycenae were built somewhat later, around 1350 to 1200 BCE. Its leaders probably controlled the whole of Argolis in this period, despite the fact that the area also contained the imposing citadels of Tiryns and Midea. However, the possibility cannot be ruled out that these centres may have controlled small territories independently of each other and that they may even have been rivals. Some researchers also believe that there could have been an alliance between them, with Mycenae playing the leading role. At this time, Greece was not a single, great empire ruled by a single dynasty, evidence of which can be found in the clay tablets containing 'Linear B' script discovered in the palace at Pylos.

Grave Circle A.

Mycenae. View from the South-West.

Archaeological research in Mycenae has confirmed that a great fire destroyed several houses to the south of Grave Circle B around 1250 BCE. Archaeologists are uncertain as to whether Mycenae was attacked by a foreign army at the time or if the fire resulted from an earthquake, but the fact remains that the fortifications were further strengthened after this event.

Towards the end of the 13th century BCE, the Mycenaean citadel was reduced to rubble. The reason for this catastrophe was not a military attack, but an earthquake. This event triggered a series of unfortunate events (including a kind of social revolution) which prevented Mycenae from ever returning to its former glory. The site was nevertheless still used, albeit with short interruptions, until historic times.

In the 8th century BCE, Argos became the dominant player in the Argolis region, although Mycenae probably retained a degree of autonomy. This continued until 468 BCE, when the Argives (who remained neutral in the conflict), jealous of the participation of Mycenaean soldiers in the wars with Persia, invaded and destroyed the city. Mycenae was rebuilt in the 3rd century BCE, but it remained firmly under the sway of Argos. The fortifications of the citadel were repaired, new temples of Athena and Hera were built on the peak of the hill and a theatre was also constructed below the fortifications. This second period of development in Mycenae was, how-

The Mask of Agamemnon.

ever, fairly short-lived, as the city was definitively abandoned in the 2nd century BCE.

The first person to focus on the ruins of Mycenae in modern times was the famous German treasure-hunter and archaeologist, Heinrich Schliemann. Whilst seeking traces of the mythical Agamemnon, Schliemann discovered the now famous Grave Circle A. He found real treasure within the graves, including gold masks (one of which was termed the Mask of Agamemnon), weaponry, ceremonial daggers, jewellery and wonderful gold and silver vessels.

The Citadel

The Citadel of Mycenae sat atop a low rock elevation protected on two sides by gorges. It was therefore only possible to enter the fortress from the west. No archaeological evidence has yet been discovered of fortification before 1350 BCE, but it cannot be ruled out that a wooden palisade or some kind of dried brick construction may have surrounded it earlier.

Imposing stone fortifications of around 900 metres in length and up to eight metres in width were constructed in three phases between 1350 and 1200 BCE. In the first phase, the fortifications ran precisely around the edges of the elevation and their remains can still be seen today on the north and south-east sides of the hill. These walls were built using 'Cyclopean' masonry techniques (the term comes from Pausanias, who believed that the fortifications here and in Tiryns must have been built by the mythical giants, the Cyclopes). Massive, roughly worked blocks of local limestone created the inner and outer faces of the walls, which were filled in with earth and rubble.

Around 1250 BCE, the fortifications of Mycenae were expanded to the south-west. At this time, the magnificent Lion Gate and the North Gate (also known as the Postern Gate) were built to the north of the Citadel. Ashlar masonry techniques (precisely shaped rectangular stone blocks placed in regular rows) were employed in the construction of the walls near to the Lion Gate. It must be admitted that they still look highly impressive today,

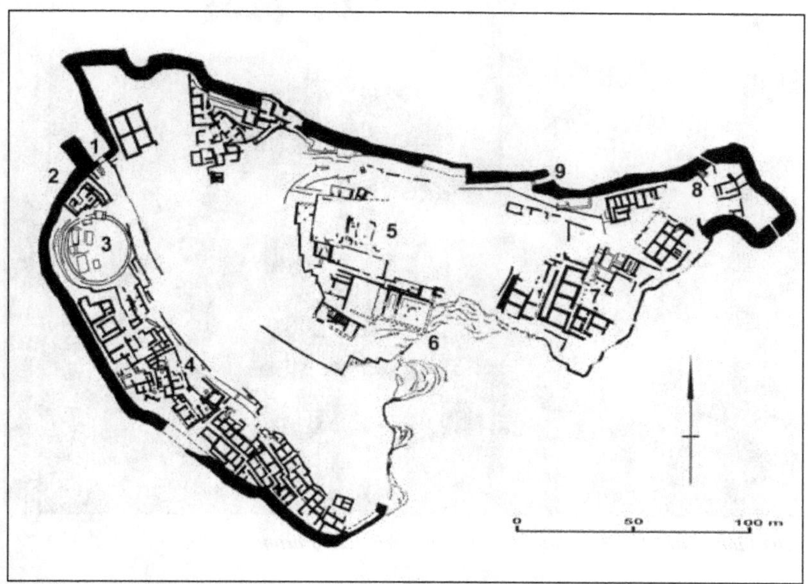

Plan of the Citadel: 1 – Lion Gate, 2 – Granary, 3 – Grave Circle A, 4 – Cult Centre, 5 – Palace, 6 – Megaron, 7 – House of Columns, 8 – Underground Cistern, 9 – Postern Gate (after Iakovidis 1983, plan 4).

especially when we consider that the walls would have reached ten metres in height in Mycenaean times.

The third phase of construction of the fortifications occurred towards the end of the 13th century BCE. At the time, the North-East Extension was added, ensuring access to an underground water cistern.

Close to the Lion Gate, it is also possible to see sections of wall built using polygonal masonry, which causes the face of the wall to resemble a honeycomb. This pattern comes from Hellenistic times, however, when the Mycenaean fortifications were being repaired for a newly-created settlement.

There still remain, however, parts of the city wall, including the gate, upon which stand lions. (Pausanias: 2.16.5)

Cyclopean walls next to the Lion Gate. West.

The Lion Gate. The 'relieving triangle' with relief decoration.

In Mycenaean times, a steep ramp, flanked to the left by the walls of the fortress and to the right by an intentionally protruding bastion (which was created to pose further difficulty to attacking armies), led up to the Lion Gate, the main entrance to the Citadel. The gate itself consisted of four massive stone blocks, each weighing around twenty tonnes. Preserved openings in the threshold and lintel indicate that a double wooden gateway once stood here.

The Interior of the Citadel: The Granary (on the left) and the Lion Gate (on the right).

A marvellous limestone slab with a relief decoration depicting two lions was placed above the lintel in the form of a 'relieving triangle'. The heads of the lions, which would have been made of bronze or gold, have unfortunately not survived to our times. The lions stand with their front paws resting on two altars and a single column in between them, which probably represented a palace or a centre of rule. In its entirety, it would have symbolised the political, military and economic might of the leaders of Mycenae.

Just after the Lion Gate on the right are the remains of the Granary. It was a two-storey complex, of which only the ground floor (consisting of several small rooms) has survived. It was built during the expansion of the fortifications around 1250 BCE and was probably originally a guardhouse. Its current name was given to it by archaeologists who found numerous vessels containing charred barley and wheat grains on its premises. However, these date to the Late Helladic IIIC period, the time when the tragic earthquake of around 1200 BCE occurred. For this reason, the Granary is believed by many archaeologists to be the longest used building after the fall of Mycenae in the Late Bronze Age.

Grave Circle A lies a little further on from the Granary and was discovered in the 19th century by Heinrich Schliemann. In 1956, excavation work was still being conducted here by the Greek archaeologist, Ioannis Papadimi-

The Grave Circle A.

Shaft graves inside Grave Circle A.

triou. Initially, the circle lay outside the Citadel, but after the expansion of the fortifications around 1250 BCE, it lay within its perimeter. A wall made of limestone slabs with a parapet (still visible today) was also created at this time, which replaced an earlier enclosure made of unworked stones. The diameter of Circle A is around 28 metres. During the course of their research, Schliemann and Papadimitriou discovered six family graves dating to the years between 1600 and 1450 BCE. They were made up of a rectangular entry shaft with a funerary chamber lying below. The two sections were separated by stone slabs. A total of nineteen people were buried here, including men, women and children. The dead were placed directly onto the floor of the funerary chamber and wonderful gifts were then placed around them. After the funeral ceremony was completed, the entry shaft was filled in with earth and a stone stele was placed above to indicate the positioning of the grave. The steles were covered in relief decoration bearing abstract geometric patterns and figural scenes of battle and hunting. Researchers still dispute to this day whether the circle was filled over with an earth tumulus or if it was flat. Amongst the grave furnishing discovered by Schliemann were many marvellous objects, including a famous gold mask, weapons, ceremonial daggers, jewellery, and gold and silver vessels. These can all now be seen at the National Archaeological Museum in Athens.

To the south-east of Grave Circle A, the remains of a series of houses constructed in the 13th and 12th centuries BCE can be seen (the Ramp House, the House of the Warrior Vase, the South House and the Tsountas House). A 'cult centre' lies between them, but this is currently covered by a roof and off limits to tourists. It consisted of several small rooms which are now believed to have formed a temple. During research conducted here, archaeologists have come across wonderful wall frescos, parts of a cult statue (the head of a woman made of stucco) and also numerous terracotta figures, which are now exhibited at the National Archaeological Museum of Athens and the Archaeological Museum of Nafplio.

From below Grave Circle A, we now follow a comfortable path made for tourists towards the peak of the Citadel. It was here at the very summit that the palace of the leader, which dominated the Citadel, was built. Beautiful views of the whole area stretch out from here over the whole region. Unfortunately, the Mycenae Palace was irrevocably destroyed in later times and only a section of it, believed by the majority of researchers to have been its central megaron, has survived to our times.

The palace was entered from the north-west at the end of a path leading from the Lion Gate and the North Gate. After passing through a small propylon, you would have found yourself in a corridor leading to a paved courtyard (twelve by fifteen metres), from which it would have been possible to directly enter the megaron. The megaron had measurements of 11.5 by 23 metres and consisted of a two-columned portico, a small vestibule and a main room known as the 'throne room'. Within the throne room, there

The Megaron. The remains of the hearth are under the temporary roof.

was a hearth surrounded by four columns which supported a roof. The walls of the megaron would have been decorated with frescos presenting battle scenes, whilst the floor would have been laid with gypsum slabs.

Unfortunately, not much has survived of the palace rooms located to the north of the megaron, as it was here that two temples, one Archaic and one Hellenistic, were constructed in later times. Some researchers believe that royal apartments were located here, whilst others suggest that this was in fact the location of the central megaron of the palace, where the leader granted his guests an audience.

After familiarising ourselves with the remains of the palace, we now move further east in the direction of the Lower Terrace, where the remains of the House of Columns can be seen. It is now considered to have been part of the eastern section of the palace, which was used for the manufacture of goods. Workshops of highly qualified artisans were located in its neighbouring rooms.

In the ruins of Mycenae is a fountain called Persea; ... (Pausanias: 2.16.6)

The small North-East Extension of the Citadel, to which we now turn, was built at the end of the 13th century BCE and would have served as protection for the underground cistern which was located here. This ensured that the city had a supply of water, even if the Citadel was placed under siege by an enemy army. Rock-cut steps led below the defensive wall then changed

The North-East Extension of the Citadel.

direction several times before finally reaching the rock-cut tanks (lined with plaster), which were topped up by water from a nearby source via terracotta pipes. If you have a torch, it is worth venturing down the steps to see this unique masterpiece of Mycenaean engineering.

After visiting the cistern, we now move along an alleyway which leads along the northern walls of the Citadel to the previously mentioned North Gate, sometimes also termed the Postern Gate. From here, moving further west, we come to an alleyway we have already seen which leads towards Grave Circle A and the Lion Gate. Alternatively, we can head directly from the North Gate to the small Archaeological Museum lying to the north of the Citadel.

The entrance to the underground cistern.

The Postern Gate.

The Lower City, the Necropolis and the Archaeological Museum

The Lower City, the Necropolis, Grave Circle B and the mighty Tholos Tombs (dating from 1500 to 1250 BCE) are all located outside the area of the Citadel.

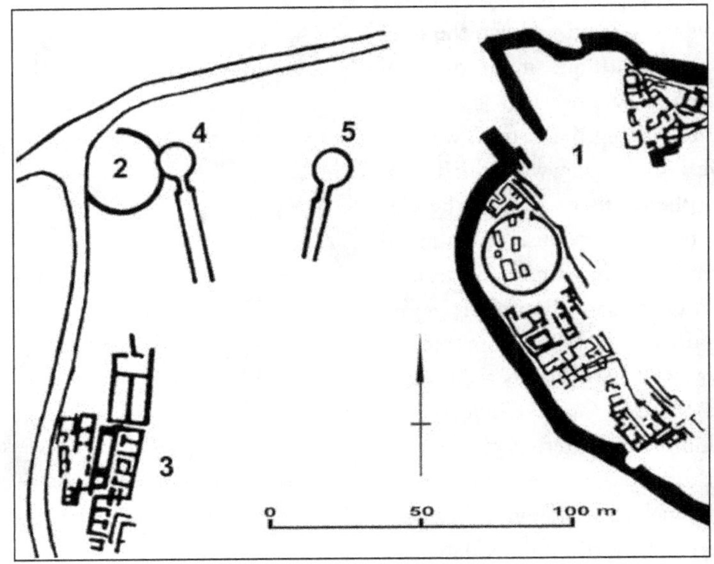

Plan of the surroundings of the Citadel: 1 – Citadel, 2 – Grave Circle B, 3 – Houses, 4 – Tomb of Clytemnestra, 5 – Tomb of Aegisthus (after Iakovidis 1998, p. 48).

However, before we venture to these sites, it is first worth visiting the small Archaeological Museum mentioned above, within which objects from the excavations of Mycenae and its surrounding area are collected. Unfortunately, the most impressive finds of H. Schliemann are currently displayed in the National Archaeological Museum of Athens rather than here.

Grave Circle B, which is located just next to the car park and the ticket office, was discovered and investigated in the 1950s by the Greek archaeologists, Ioannis Papadimitriou and Georgios Mylonas. As was the case with the previously described Grave Circle A, it had a diameter of approximately 28 metres. Little has survived of the wall (peribolos) which once surrounded it and we do not know if the peribolos supported an earth tumulus or if it simply lay on level ground.

26 graves have been discovered in Grave Circle B, the majority of which are shaft graves, scattered across the circle without any specific orientation or sign of intentional grouping. The burials discovered within them were dated by archaeologists to a period between 1650 and 1500 BCE. The some-

what smaller measurements of the graves and their more modest furnishing indicates that members of the first dynasty of Mycenaean leaders were buried here, with this circle later being succeeded by Grave Circle A as the burial site of the elite.

In the past, most researchers considered Grave Circle B to be of less importance than Grave Circle A, considering the lesser furnishing of the graves to be evidence of the lower status of those buried within. Indeed, the largest and most richly furnished grave of Circle B only comes close to the poorest grave of Circle A in terms of construction and the riches it contained. However, it is now believed that this difference is due to the increasing affluence of the Mycenaeans and not due to a difference in social rank between the dead buried in the two circles.

In fact, we can be certain that the dead buried in Circle B belonged to the elite of their time, since they left many valuable items underlining their social status. Amongst these objects, a vessel made of a single piece of rock crystal with a handle in the shape of a goose's head is of particular interest. It is now exhibited at the National Archaeological Museum of Athens.

Differences emerge, however, in the later treatment of the circles. Circle A was left practically untouched as its surroundings were reorganised and it was incorporated into the zone of the Mycenaean Citadel halfway through the 13th century BCE. Circle B, on the other hand, was first disturbed by grave 'P' halfway through the 15th century BCE and was then completely disregarded during the construction of the mighty Tomb of Clytemnestra, which was probably built towards the end of the 14th century BCE.

Grave Circle B.

Houses outside the Citadel.

To the south of Grave Circle B, it is possible to see the remains of four living quarters which have been investigated by archaeologists: the West House, the House of the Shields, the House of the Oil Merchant and the House of the Sphinxes. All date to the 13th century BCE. During research conducted in the 1950s and 1960s, finds discovered here included numerous olive oil storage vessels, luxury items made of ivory, faience and stone and tablets with Linear B script, all of which suggest that these complexes were used as houses.

...there are also underground chambers of Atreus and his children, in which were stored their treasures. There is the grave of Atreus, along with the graves of such as returned with Agamemnon from Troy, ... Agamemnon has his tomb, ... Clytemnestra and Aegisthus were buried at some little distance from the wall. (Pausanias: 2.16.6–7)

As has already been mentioned, Grave Circle B was disturbed in a later period during the construction of the imposing tholos tomb known as the Tomb of Clytemnestra. It was one of nine tombs of the type built in the surroundings of Mycenae. Tholos tombs (sometimes also known as beehive tombs) consisted of a long corridor (dromos), a small mouth passage (stomion) and a round chamber covered by something like a dome. Due to differences in the architectural traits of the tholos tombs constructed in the necropolis of Mycenae, they have been divided into three groups. The first

The Tomb of Clytemnestra with one row of seats of the Hellenistic theatre in the foreground.

group consists of the Cyclopean Tomb, the Tomb of Aegisthus and Epano Phournos. The Lion Tomb, the Panagia Tomb and Kato Phournos make up the second, whilst the third group, containing the most impressive tholoi, comprises the Tomb of the Genii, the Tomb of Clytemnestra and the Tomb

The Epano Phournos Tomb.

The Tomb of Aegisthus

of Agamemnon (also known as the Treasury of Atreus). The names of all these tombs are, of course, invented, as they were assigned by contemporary researchers of the Mycenae site.

The tholoi of the first group were built of unworked stone or only slightly modified stone blocks. They possessed neither a relieving triangle above the entrance nor regular walls along the sides of the dromos. These traits can be seen in the Tomb of Aegisthus (just next to the entrance to the Citadel), which was built around 1500 BCE.

The Lion Tomb.

The second group of tholoi were built of worked stone blocks with wrought stomia, a relieving triangle above the entrance and properly constructed walls within the dromos. An example of this group is the Lion Tomb (from around 1450 BCE), which can be found on the path to the local Archaeological Museum.

Tholoi belonging to the third group are characterised by their considerably larger size. They are made of wonderfully worked stone

The Tomb of Agamemnon.

blocks, possess façades decorated with reliefs in the entrance to the stomia and have closed wooden doors. The two most impressive tholoi of this group are unquestionably worth visiting. These are the Tomb of Clytemnestra (next to the Tomb of Aegisthus) and the Tomb of Agamemnon (situated not far from the Citadel, on the main road leading to the archaeological site).

The Tomb of Agamemnon was built around 1400 BCE. The dromos which leads to it is 36 metres long and is lined by ashlar walls. Just before

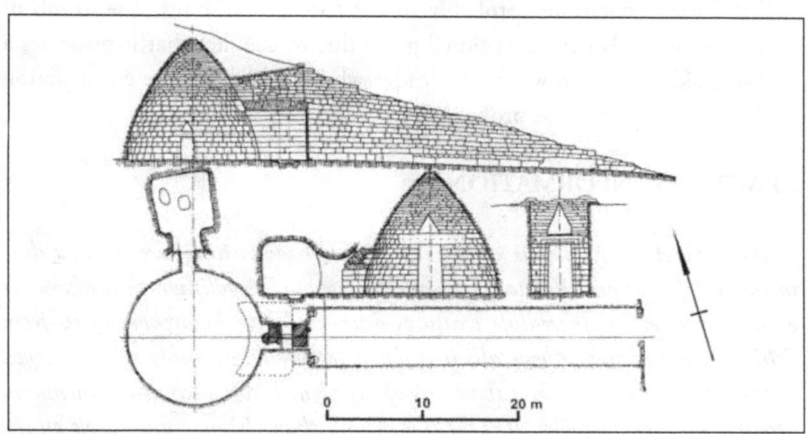

Plan and section of the Tomb of Agamemnon (after Dinsmoor 1975, fig. 13).

The Tomb of Agamemnon. Inside view with the entrance to the side chamber.

the entrance to the dromos are the remains of the wall which once blocked its entrance. It was the custom for the Mycenaeans to fill in the dromos and tomb once the funerary ceremonies were completed and the Tomb of Agamemnon was no exception to this rule. This was carried out despite the fact that it possessed a wonderfully decorated, elevated entrance stomion. Its massive, closed double doors were flanked by half columns made of green marble and the triangular space above the lintel was occupied by a slab of red marble decorated with spirals, also flanked by half columns.

The wonderfully preserved, curved funerary chamber itself has a diameter of over fourteen metres and is thirteen metres high. Despite the fact that Argolis was plagued with powerful earthquakes, it was never destroyed. Bronze rivets found here by archaeologists indicate that it was once adorned with bronze decorations, probably in the forms of rosettes. The Tomb of Agamemnon is also an exceptional grave due to the fact that it possesses a rock-cut side chamber, where the leader who had ordered the construction of this mighty tholos was probably laid to rest.

PRACTICAL INFORMATION:

The Citadel of Mycenae is a place which everybody visiting Greece has a duty to see. This is not only due to the wonderful views of Argolis which it affords or even because of the incredible treasures discovered here by archaeologists from Schliemann onwards. Above all, it is down to the unbelievably well-preserved nature of constructions from the times of mythical heroes such as Agamemnon, Orestes and even Heracles. It is for this reason, that Mycenae finds itself on the UNESCO world heritage list.

It may come as a surprise, but Mycenae is best visited in late autumn or even in winter, since it is then possible to contemplate its wonderful sights in complete solitude. In the high season, which runs from early spring to late autumn, many organised tours make their way through the site. In Mycenae, the most important sights are as follows:

- The Lion Gate and its adjacent fortifications
- Grave Circle A (shaft graves)
- The Palace Remains (including the megaron of the king)
- The Rear (Eastern) Section of the Citadel (including the underground cistern)
- The Tomb of Agamemnon (also known as the Treasury of Atreus)

With a little more time on your hands, the following are also worthy of your attention: The Cult Centre, The Postern (North) Gate, The Tomb of Clytemnestra, The Tomb of Aegisthus and The Lion Tomb

In addition, it is worth considering a visit to the small Archaeological Museum, which contains a collection of exhibits from excavations conducted in Mycenae and the surrounding area. However, the most impressive objects discovered by H. Schliemann are now housed in the National Archaeological Museum of Athens.

The ruins of 'Agamemnon's Fortress' are located close to the modern village of Mycenae. It is possible to travel here by car from Athens (one-and-a-half hours) or Nafplio (thirty minutes) without any real difficulty. The city of Nafplio is, in fact, an excellent base for visiting all of Argolis. Mycenae can also be reached by train, but the journey to the archaeological site entails either a walk of several kilometres or a short taxi ride.

Archaeological Site and the Museum:

Open: *1 April – 31 October: Monday-Sunday: 8 a.m. – 8 p.m.*
1 November – 31 March: Monday-Sunday: 8 a.m. – 3 p.m.
Tickets: *Full – 8 Euros; Reduced – 4 Euros*
Special ticket package valid for the Archaeological Site, the Museum and the Treasury of Atreus: Full – 8 Euros; Reduced – 4 Euros
Free admission days: *6 March 18 April 18 May 5 June, 28 October, the last weekend of September, every first Sunday from November 1st to March 31st*
Site closed: *1 January, 25 March, Easter Sunday, 1 May, 25–26 December*

It should be remembered that many people (from member states of the European Union) are entitled to free entry to the archaeological sites of Greece. This includes those over 65 or under 18, students and academic instructors.

It is always worth checking at the entrance about the possibility of a discount to the ticket price. A website prepared by the Greek Ministry of Tourism is also of assistance in this matter: http://odysseus.culture.gr/index_en.html

The Tholos in the Sanctuary of Asclepius.

EPIDAURUS

At Lessa the Argive territory joins that of Epidaurus. But before you reach Epidaurus itself you will come to the sanctuary of Asclepius. (Pausanias: 2.26.1)

The ancient city of Epidaurus was located on the Saronic Gulf in eastern Argolis. Port installations, acropolis fortifications, a theatre dating to the 4th–3rd century BCE and the remains of Roman houses (near the agora) have all survived to our times. To the west of the port, archaeologists have discovered traces of a small sanctuary of Artemis from the Archaic period. However, the remains of the sanctuaries of Asclepius and Apollo Maleatas (the Healer), located close to Epidaurus, are of far more interest.

The sacred grove of Asclepius is surrounded on all sides by boundary marks. (Pausanias: 2.27.1)

According to Greek myth, Asclepius was the son of the god, Apollo, and a royal daughter by the name of Coronis. After the death of his mother, he was raised on Mount Pelion by the centaur, Chiron, who taught him the art of healing the sick. After some time, Asclepius was then accepted into the community of the Greek gods. According to Pausanias, however, Coronis, fearing the anger of her lawful husband, Phlegyas, left the small Asclepius on Mount Titthium, where he was looked after by a dog and fed by one of the goats of the shepherd, Aresthanas.

In antiquity, the most famous cult place of Asclepius lay in a broad valley within the territory of the city of Epidaurus and the beginnings of his sanctuary date back to the 6th century BCE. The cult of Asclepius is now believed to have been brought to Argolis most probably from Messene or Thessaly, but the erstwhile residents of Epidaurus claimed that the birthplace of the god was to be found here.

At the beginning of the 4th century BCE, the sanctuary became a place of pilgrimage for numerous invalids from all over Greece and the citizens of Epidaurus thus embarked on a massive construction project to build a more impressive sanctuary dedicated to 'their' god.

The cult of Asclepius in Epidaurus was so popular that people travelled from as far as Rome at the beginning of the 3rd century BCE. This did not, however, prevent the army of General Sulla from looting the sanctuary in around 86 BCE. In a later period, making use of the Pax Romana, the sanctuary enjoyed another period of prosperity, which resulted in further construction projects (above all in the 2nd century CE), partially funded

The Theatre of Epidaurus.

by Senator Antoninus, a rich aristocrat from the western part of Asia Minor.

Around halfway through the 3rd century CE, due to the threat of attack by foreign armies, a defensive wall was built around the sanctuary, which included elements taken from earlier buildings within it. A church was built near the northern entrance to the sanctuary at the end of the 4th century CE, which is now one of the oldest Christian churches in Greece. As was the case with so many other places of the kind, the end of the Sanctuary of Asclepius at Epidaurus came as a result of the decree of Emperor Theodosius I, who in 394 CE prohibited the functioning of all pagan cult places within the territory of his empire.

Archaeological excavation at Epidaurus was begun in 1881 by Greek researchers, who continued their work until 1928. Further research was then supervised by members of the French School of Athens between 1942 and 1943, whilst workers of the Greek Archaeological Service conducted research within the famous theatre from 1954 to 1963. Today, work is being carried out within the archaeological park on the reconstruction of the most important buildings of the Sanctuary of Asclepius.

The Theatre

A visit to the sanctuary is best begun in the small archaeological museum, which can be found on the way from the entrance gate to the theatre. It contains pieces of architectural decoration from the most important buildings

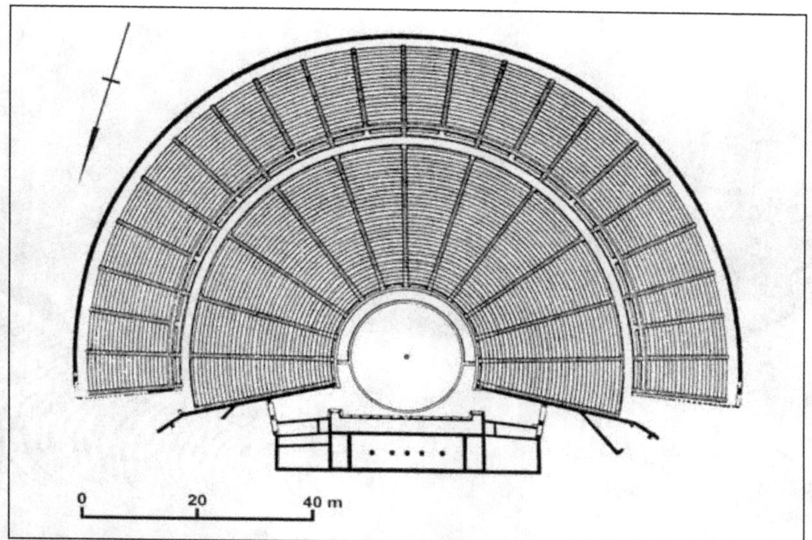

Plan of the Theatre of Epidaurus (after Dinsmoor 1975, fig. 90)

(the tholos and the temples of Asclepius and Artemis), as well as numerous examples of sculptures and pottery vessels found during the course of excavations. The remainder of the objects discovered here are exhibited in the National Archaeological Museum in Athens.

The Epidaurians have a theatre within the sanctuary, in my opinion very well worth seeing. (Pausanias: 2.27.5)

Just next to the museum building, to the south-east of the Sanctuary of Asclepius, stands one of the best preserved theatres of ancient Greece. It was probably built around 330–320 BCE and initially possessed 34 rows of stone seating divided into twelve sectors intended for around 6,000 spectators. The auditorium rested entirely on a natural hill.

In the 2nd century BCE, the upper part of the auditorium was given an additional 21 rows of seating, which were divided into 22 sectors. It was now necessary for part of the auditorium to be supported by an artificially created hill and side retaining walls. After this expansion, the theatre could hold up to 12,000 spectators. The first row of seating was for the most important guests and differed from the rest in that it was made of red limestone and had back support. The orchestra had a diameter of 20.3 metres and was made of beaten earth, surrounded by a stone circle of marble slabs. An altar (*thymele*) stood in the centre of it.

The Theatre of Epidaurus.

Unfortunately, the skene has barely survived to our times. It was probably around 26 metres long and flanked by two side rooms. On the side of the auditorium was a proskenion, the façade of which was adorned with fourteen Ionic columns. Two passages (*parodoi*) ran between the orchestra and the skene leading to the auditorium.

The Theatre of Epidaurus was mainly used for dramatic spectacles and musical competitions of the festival which took place here every four years (the Asclepieia). It is worth remembering that theatrical plays and musical concerts still take place here today and if you decide to pretend to be an ancient actor standing in the middle of the auditorium, you cannot fail to be amazed by the acoustics. (In ancient times, however, the actors would have stood on the elevated stage behind the auditorium known as the proskenion).

The Sanctuary of Asclepius

Our visit to the Sanctuary of Asclepius begins in its south-eastern section (currently to the north of the museum), where the remains of a large building in the shape of a square with sides of 76 metres dating to the beginning of the 3rd century BCE can be found. It was probably a kind of hotel (*xenon*)

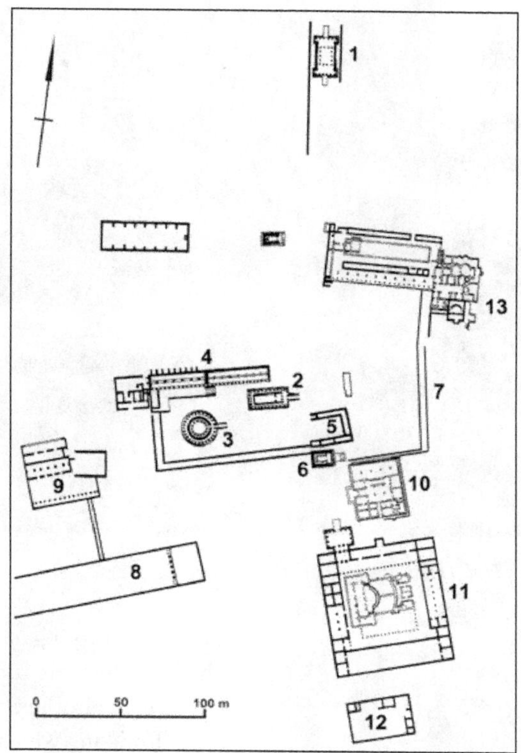

Plan of the Sanctuary of Asclepius: 1 – Propylae, 2 – Temple of Asclepius, 3 – Tholos, 4 – Abaton, 5 – Building E, 6 – Temple of Artemis, 7 – Fortifications, 8 – Stadium, 9 – Palaestra, 10 – Roman building, 11 – Hestiatorion, 12 – Hellenistic Baths, 13 – Roman Baths (after Tomlinson 1983, p. 42).

for wealthy personages visiting the sanctuary. The complex consisted of four parts, each containing eighteen rooms situated around four inner courtyards.

Continuing west, we can soon discern a small building now known as the 'Hellenistic Baths' from the beginning of the 3rd century BCE. The remains of baths and channels transporting water to it have been discovered here.

On passing the Hellenistic Baths, we then turn right to the north where the remains of a massive building with a courtyard in its centre are visible. The whole complex had measurements of 70 by 76 metres and was probably a gigantic banqueting hall (hestiatorion) and not a gymnasium, as had previously been thought. The complex was originally entered through an imposing Doric propylaea which once stood in its northern side and which has now been partially reconstructed. The complex initially (probably in around 300 BCE) only consisted of a columned courtyard surrounded by

The Banqueting Hall (Hestiatorion).

The Propylaea through which the Banqueting Hall (Hestiatorion) was entered.

rooms of varying sizes, some of which performed the function of dining halls. In the 2nd century CE, a small odeon (which is still fairly well-preserved) was erected within the courtyard. Its actual function has not yet, however, been conclusively agreed upon by researchers.

Continuing further north, we pass a nearly square building (around 29 by 34 metres) dating to the Roman period to our right (east). Stone benches and the bases of cult statues were discovered in its central part. Researchers believe that it was probably in this place, in the 4th century CE, that the secret ceremonies of mysteries took place in honour of Asclepius, as has been attested by inscriptions discovered on the territory of the sanctuary.

Within the grove are a temple of Artemis, … a race-course consisting, like most Greek race-courses, of a bank of earth, … (Pausanias: 2.27.5)

Let us now turn our attention to the stadium situated to the west of the sanctuary. It is over 181 metres long and dates to the end of the 4th century BCE. The stone seating built on natural slopes has survived to our times (a rare occurrence in ancient Greece). The stadium was connected to the palaestra lying around fifty metres to its north by an underground tunnel.

Continuing our walk to the north towards the centre of the sanctuary, we can see the foundations of the Doric Temple of Artemis from around 330 BCE to our right (east), as well as the altar which belonged to it. The temple originally possessed six columns in its façade and a single cella, within which the statue of the goddess would have stood, surrounded by ten Corinthian columns.

To the north of the Temple of Artemis, we can see the remains of 'Building E', which dates to around 450–400 BCE. It was a relatively large complex and contained a rectangular courtyard in its centre. Some researchers believe it to have been the first shrine to be dedicated to Asclepius and that its rooms would have been used for ritual sleep.

We now come to the heart of the sanctuary, which once contained the temple of the god to whom it was dedicated. The Temple of Asclepius, the

The Stadium. View from the East.

The Temple of Aphrodite

work of the architect Theodotos, was built around 375–370 BCE. The only parts of it to survive to our times are the remains of the poros stone foundations (13.2 by 24.3 metres), sections of the floor of the pronaos and a ramp leading up to it from the east. The temple was once surrounded by a single Doric colonnade (six by eleven columns) and its entrance lay to the east up the previously mentioned small ramp. Its interior only consisted of a pronaos and a cella, in which a chryselephantine statue of Asclepius, the work of

The Temple of Asclepius (in the foreground) and the Abaton (in the background).

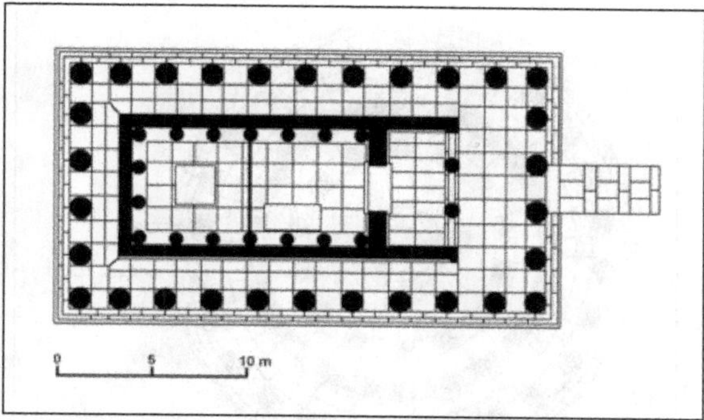

Plan of the Temple of Asclepius (after Roux 1961, pl. 28).

Thrasymedes of Paros, would once have stood. The god sat on a throne holding a sceptre in one hand with his other resting on the head of a snake. A dog was sculpted next to him.

The exterior of the temple was richly adorned by wonderful acroteria, as well as other decorations. Scenes from the Iliupersis (the Sacking of Troy) were depicted on the eastern gable and scenes from the Amazonomachy were presented on the western. To the east of the temple stood an altar, the foundations of which are still visible today.

Near [the temple of Asclepius – W.M.] has been built a circular building of white marble, called Tholos (Round House), which is worth seeing. (Pausanias: 2.27.3)

The Tholos (on the left) and the Abaton (on the right).

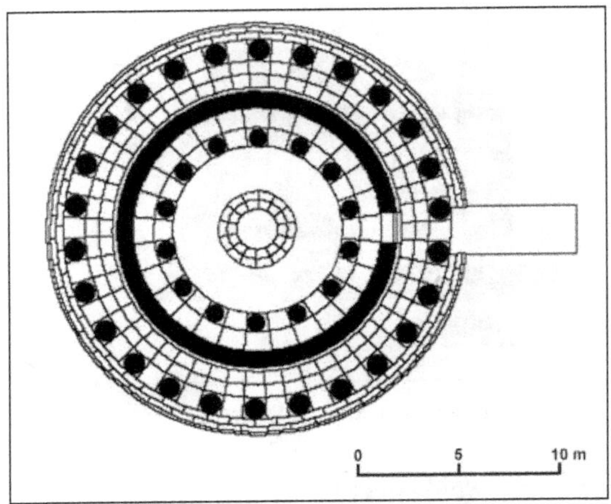

Plan of the Tholos (after Dinsmoor 1975, fig. 85).

To the south-west of the Temple of Asclepius, the round foundations of the Tholos (with a diameter of 21.82 metres) are visible. Archaeologists date the building to around 360–340 BCE and it was probably the work of the local architect, Polykleitos the Younger. It may have been a heroon of Asclepius or a place where sacrifices were made to the god.

The building is now partly restored. It was once entered via a small ramp to its east and its exterior was encircled by 26 Doric columns supporting a conical roof. The interior contained a circular room within an interior ring

The Abaton. View from the South.

of fourteen Corinthian columns. The entrance to an underground crypt was located directly in its centre. This consisted of three rings of concentric walls and was reminiscent of a labyrinth. Some researchers believe that ritual ceremonies of the Asclepius cult would have taken place here.

Over against the temple is the place where the suppliants of the god sleep. (Pausanias: 2.27.2)

To the north of the Tholos are the remains of the Abaton. It was an Ionic portico probably used as an enkoimeterion, a place dedicated to ritual sleep. Whilst dreaming, the sick were either cured or instructed what had to be done in order to return to full health. The portico was 70 metres long, 9.5 metres wide and possessed a façade with 29 Ionic columns that were connected by low balustrades.

Over the course of excavation work carried out here, archaeologists have come across two large slabs covered in inscriptions which inform us of the miracle cures (dating from around 350–300 BCE) of which Pausanias also made mention. The original Abaton (from the beginning of the 4th century BCE) was enlarged and then extended to the west in Hellenistic and Roman times.

To the north and north-east of the central part of the sanctuary, it is also possible to see the remains of its monumental entrance, Roman baths (2nd century CE), a Doric portico (beginning of the 3rd century BCE) and a huge Hellenistic cistern.

The Roman Baths. View from the South.

The North Propylaea.

Above all, it is worth visiting the ancient main entrance to the sanctuary, which led from the north through a monumental propylaea erected at the turn of the 4th and 3rd centuries BCE. The propylaea took the form of a covered rectangular hall with measurements of thirteen by twenty metres, the two narrower sides of which contained six-columned Ionic porticos and ramps leading up to them. Fourteen Corinthian columns holding up the roof stood inside.

The Sanctuary of Apollo Maleatas

Above the grove are the Nipple and another mountain called Cynortium; on the latter is a sanctuary of Maleatian Apollo. (Pausanias: 2.27.7)

Within the small Sanctuary of Apollo Maleatas, which lies on the northern slope of Mount Kynortion, archaeologists have discovered the remnants of a settlement from the Middle Bronze Age, as well as several graves. At its summit, the remains of a Mycenaean 'peak sanctuary' (1500–1200 BCE) have also survived to our times. This is a rare example on mainland Greece, as peak sanctuaries most commonly occur on Crete.

The beginnings of the cult of Apollo date to the Geometric period, but the majority of buildings come from the 4th century BCE and the period of reconstruction of the sanctuary in the 2nd century CE, which was financed by the previously mentioned Senator Antoninus. Some of the monuments to

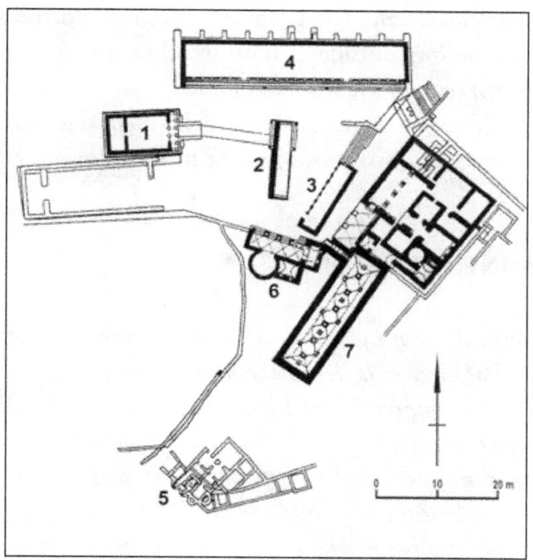

Plan of the Sanctuary of Apollo Maleatas: 1 – Temple of Apollo, 2 – Altar, 3 – Museion, 4 – Enkoimeterion, 5 – Roman Baths, 6 – Nymphaeum, 7 – Cistern.

survive to our times include the remains of a small Doric temple of Apollo from the Classical period (built on the site of an earlier Archaic temple), an altar, a temenos dedicated to the Muses and a building that was most

The Sanctuary of Asclepius. View towards Mount Kynorthion and the Sanctuary of Apollo Maleatas.

probably an enkoimeterion. The propylaea leading into the sanctuary and the complex of buildings outside its limits (baths, a nymphaeum and water-collecting cisterns) date to the Roman period.

Excavations within the Sanctuary of Apollo Maleatas have been carried out by Greek archaeologists since 1974. At present, however, it is off limits to tourists.

PRACTICAL INFORMATION:

The archaeological site of Epidaurus is currently one of the most visited tourist attractions in all of Greece. It lies in the north-eastern part of the Peloponnese near Road 70, which connects Nafplio with the modern city of Palaia Epidavros. Its location means that a trip to visit it can be combined with a visit to other interesting sites in this part of the Peloponnese such as Mycenae or Tiryns. It is easiest to reach Epidaurus by car and the journey from Athens (140km) should take approximately two hours. However, a much better option is to visit it from Nafplio, which is a most useful base for visiting numerous sites in the north-eastern Peloponnese (Corinth, Nemea, Mycenae, Argos, Tiryns and others). From Nafplio (30km), Epidaurus can be reached in around half an hour. A large, shaded car park is located just in front of the entrance to the site.

Your walk around the site should begin in the small museum not far from the entrance. Admittedly, the most interesting objects discovered in Epidaurus are now on display at the National Archaeological Museum of Athens, but the local museum nevertheless possesses an interesting collection that includes elements of architectonic decoration and marble statues from the Roman period.

The biggest attraction of Epidaurus is without doubt its wonderful theatre, the best preserved example of its kind in Greece.

After visiting the theatre, about an hour-and-a-half should be allotted to a peaceful stroll amongst the remains of the former Sanctuary of Asclepius. Of the numerous preserved buildings to be found here, particular attention should be paid to the Tholos (now partially reconstructed), the Temple of Asclepius, the Abaton (where the infirm awaited miracle cures), the Stadium and the Propylaea (monumental gate) that once led into the sanctuary itself.

Sanctuary of Asclepius and Archaeological Museum:

Open:

1 April – 31 October:
Monday-Sunday: 8 a.m. – 8 p.m.
1 November – 31 March:
Monday-Sunday: 8 a.m. – 6 p.m.

Tickets: *Full – 6 Euros; Reduced – 3 Euros*
Special ticket package valid for both the archaeological site and the museum: Full – 6 Euros; Reduced – 3 Euros
Free admission days: *6 March, 18 April, 18 May, 5 June, 28 October, the last weekend of September, every first Sunday from November 1st to March 31st*
Site closed: *1 January, 25 March, Easter Sunday, 1 May, 25–26 December*

It should be remembered that many people (from member states of the European Union) are entitled to free entry to the archaeological sites of Greece. This includes those over 65 or under 18, students and academic instructors.

It is always worth checking at the entrance about the possibility of a discount to the ticket price. A website prepared by the Greek Ministry of Tourism is also of assistance in this matter: http://odysseus.culture.gr/index_en.html

Corinthian capital at Epidauros Archaeological Museum.

Menelaion. Part of Mansion 2.

SPARTA AND MENELAION

Farther on from Thornax is the city, which was originally named Sparta, but in course of time came to be called Lacedaemon as well, a name which till then belonged to the land. (Pausanias: 3.11.1)

After visiting Argolis and the island of Aegina, Pausanias moved south in the direction of Laconia and its capital, the once mighty Sparta, which was the second most important city of ancient Greece after Athens. Sparta is located in pretty much the centre of Laconia, in the valley of the river Eurotas, which flows to the east of the imposing Taygetus mountain range.

The surroundings of Sparta were first settled either towards the end of the Neolithic period or at the beginning of the Early Bronze Age (see Menelaion below). However, people probably only began living on the site of the later city from around the 10th century BCE. These people came from outside Laconia, spoke a Doric dialect and quickly became the dominant force in the region after conquering first the nearby Amyclae and then the remainder of Laconia around 750 BCE. In the period between the 6th and 4th centuries BCE, the Spartans, as leaders of a military alliance covering the whole of the Peloponnese, became the most powerful political and military force in Greece. Thanks to their alliance with Persia (which included financial backing), they won the final victory of the seemingly endless Peloponnesian Wars by decisively defeating the Athenians in 404 BCE.

Soon afterwards, however, after being defeated by the armies of Thebes in the Battle of Leuctra, the importance of Sparta in the Greek world began to diminish. Internal problems caused by attempts at social reform (3rd century BCE) continued to plague the city until the period of rule of the last king of Sparta, Nabis (207–192 BCE).

In Roman times, Sparta experienced a second heyday as a free city under the control of Rome. It probably avoided attack by the Heruli (268 CE), but it was later destroyed by the army of Alaric (396 CE), an event that prompted its inhabitants to build a new set of walls. Sparta was also the seat of a bishop in the 5th and 6th centuries CE.

One of the first to try to find the remains of the ancient city of Sparta was Heinrich Schliemann, who was naturally most keen to discover the mythical palace of King Menelaus. However, as he himself expressed in his diaries, he did not come across so much as the remains of a refuse dump whilst digging at the Spartan acropolis. The first excavation work to bear fruit was led by Charles Waldstein of the American School of Classical Studies of Athens in the years 1892 and 1893. Subsequent excavations were then overseen by researchers of the British Archaeological School of Athens; these took place between 1906 and 1910, from 1924 to 1928 and finally in 1949. After a long hiatus, British archaeologists reconvened their research of Sparta in the 1990s. It should also be mentioned that Greek archaeologists conducted a small-scale excavation (as well as rescue excavations) in the area of the modern day city in 1957.

Archaeological work thus far has mainly focused on the area of the acropolis and the northern section of the city. It has not yet provided us with satisfactory answers concerning the location of the most important buildings of ancient Sparta, including those which were mentioned by Pausanias.

The Centre of Ancient Sparta

There are, however, hills in the city, and the highest of them they call the citadel. Here is built a sanctuary of Athena, who is called both City-protecting and Lady of the Bronze House. (Pausanias: 3.17.1–2)

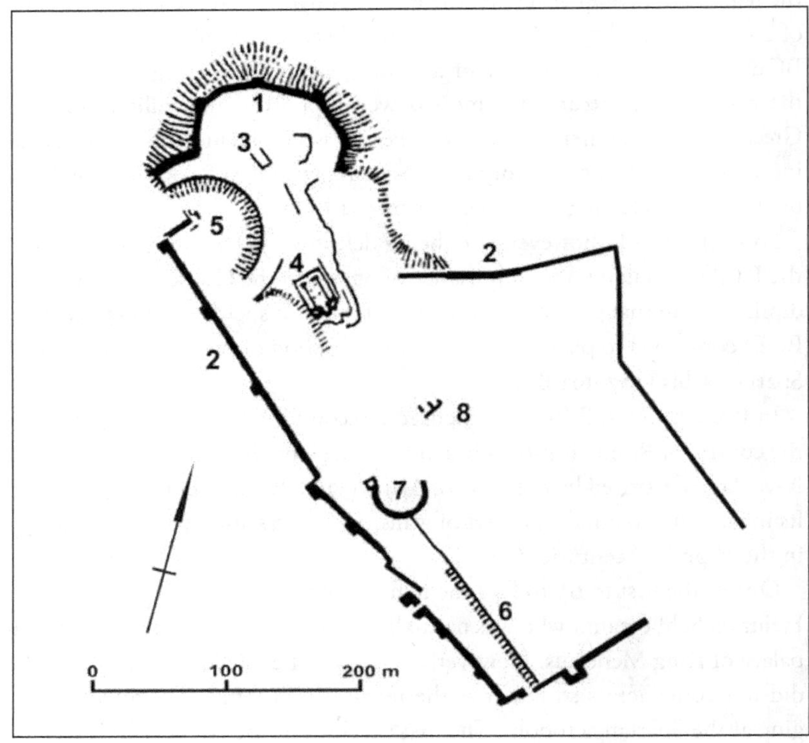

Plan of Sparta: 1 – Acropolis, 2 – Fortifications, 3 – Temple of Athena, 4 – Church, 5 – Theatre, 6 – Portico, 7 – Round Building, 8 – Agora (?) (after Waywell 2010, Figure 1).

One would assume that a plethora of interesting constructions would have survived from a city as wonderful as ancient Sparta, but a visit to the archaeological site today may prove disappointing for some. In comparison to Athens, Corinth and even Argos, very few buildings have weathered the storms of time.

The centre of ancient Sparta was its acropolis, which now lies to the north of the modern city amongst vast olive groves. The majority of ancient constructions which have been preserved, however, come from later Roman and Byzantine times, including sections of the mighty fortifications which date to the end of the 4th century CE.

In possession of a brilliant army and naturally fortified by the mighty mountain range surrounding it, Sparta had no need of defensive walls before the end of the Classical period. In the Hellenistic period, however, when Spartan power began to wane, imposing fortifications of dried brick were constructed on top of stone foundations (end of the 3rd to the beginning of the 2nd centuries BCE). These remains have lasted until today in several places within the modern day city and it is clear that they would have protected a massive, practically oval area lying between the Eurotas and Magoula rivers. Sparta functioned within these fortifications until 396 CE.

After the destruction of the existing defences by the army of Alaric, new stone fortifications were built. Many elements of earlier (Classical or Hellenistic) buildings were employed in their construction. The new wall, which protected a considerably reduced area of the city in comparison to its predecessor, still encompassed the Spartan acropolis and was repaired several times in later periods. These fortifications are particularly well preserved on the south-western side of the acropolis, between the Roman portico and the theatre.

The remains of the Temple of Athena Chalkioikos.

At the peak of the acropolis, it is possible to see the poorly preserved foundations of the Temple of Athena Chalkioikos ('Lady of the

Bronze House'), which date to the second half of the 6th century BCE. The moniker derives from the bronze bas-reliefs and reliefs which once adorned it. Furthermore, a bronze statue of the goddess by the local artist, Gitiadas, once stood within the temple. An earlier shrine was previously located on the same site, which dates to the 8th century BCE.

Archaeological research conducted to the south of the Temple of Athena has uncovered the remains of a small portico, which is probably the one mentioned by Pausanias as belonging to the Temple of Athena Ergane (Protector of Artisans). It was during excavation work here that a famous fragment of a Late Archaic marble hoplite statue was discovered, which is thought to have been of Leonidas. It is currently on display in the archaeological museum in the centre of Sparta.

To the west of the Temple of Athena are the remains of an early church (5th to 7th centuries CE), which is one of five discovered thus far by archaeologists in Sparta.

On going westwards from the market-place is a cenotaph of Brasidas the son of Tellis. Not far from it is the theatre, made of white marble and worth seeing. Opposite the theatre are two tombs; the first is that of Pausanias, the general at Plataea, the second is that of Leonidas. (Pausanias: 3.14.1)

On the south-west slope of the acropolis are the remains of the Roman theatre. Built around 30–20 BCE, it was once adorned with slabs and decoration made of local marble and it made a great impression on Pausanias.

Early Byzantine church on the acropolis in Sparta.

The Theatre of Sparta.

The theatre of Sparta was indeed a magnificent construction, based as it was on Late Classical Greek theatres, such as those found in Megalopolis and Epidaurus. The semi-circular viewing area (*cavea* in Latin) had a diameter of 114 metres and was divided into upper and lower sections by a central passageway (*praecinctio* in Latin), which could be entered via external steps on the side of the eastern entrance (*parodos* in Greek).

The upper part of the viewing gallery consisted of sixteen sectors containing seventeen rows of seats, whilst the lower contained nine sectors with 31 rows of seats. Below the auditorium was a circular orchestra with a diameter of 25.52 metres. In 1997, British archaeologists discovered evidence that the original stage of the theatre (prob-

Part of the auditorium of the theatre.

The remains of the scenae frons in the theatre.

ably made of wood and measuring 9 by 34 metres) was placed on wheels and that it was possible to move it up and down the side of the western entrance in order to change the set (*skenotheke* in Greek). In 78 CE, during the rule of Emperor Vespasian, a classical Roman permanent stage with a Corinthian façade (*scenae frons* in Latin) was installed during the reconstruction of the theatre.

The eastern retaining wall of the theatre.

The Spartans used the theatre for classical plays, football competitions between two teams of young Spartans and probably also for political meetings. On the eastern wall (which supported the auditorium), 37 inscriptions were carved between 80 and 180 CE. These included lists of names of the people chosen each year to form the local political council, as well as descriptions of individual careers. This was the case with a certain Eudocimus, whose inscription drew attention to the fact that he was particularly proud that, during his three missions to buy grain for the city, he had not thrown any of the sacks overboard to rescue his ship in storms.

The most striking feature in the marketplace is the portico which they call Persian because it was made from spoils taken in the Persian wars. (Pausanias: 3.11.3)

The southern section of the acropolis also contains the ruins (fenced off and currently off limits) of a great Roman portico dating to the rule of Emperor Hadrian. Archaeological research has shown that the portico was a building on two floors with a length of around 200 metres and that it was made of brick, whilst its floor was laid with coloured marble. The 24 covered rooms in its lower floor were probably used as shops and its southern and eastern sides were fronted by Corinthian colonnades. Some researchers now believe that this construction was the Persian portico described by Pausanias.

The 'Circular Building'.

By the Canopy is a circular building, and in it images of Zeus and Aphrodite surnamed Olympian. (Pausanias: 3.12.11)

The remains of a round building, which has been identified by some researchers as the 'circular building' (erected by Epimenides of Crete and containing statues of Zeus and Aphrodite) described by Pausanias, can be discerned to the west of the portico. It was originally an earth mound surrounded by a circular wall in the Hellenistic period, before it was later rebuilt in Roman times. After reconstruction, its circular foundations supported an open colonnade, within which marble sculptures were placed. Certain archaeologists, however, believe that this round building was the Cenotaph of Brasidas (one of the commanders of the Spartan army in the Peloponnesian Wars), which Pausanias also mentioned.

The remains of the Agora (?).

The Lacedaemonians who live in Sparta have a market-place worth seeing; the council-chamber of the senate, and the offices of the ephors, of the guardians of the laws, and of those called the Bidiaeans, are all in the market-place. (Pausanias: 3.11.2)

Thus far, archaeologists have not yet managed to decide upon the site of the main square of Sparta, which constituted its agora. Two theories exist as to its whereabouts, although neither has been conclusively proved. The first contends that it lay on the fairly flat land located to the south of the Roman portico, outside the later defensive walls of the city and under the modern stadium. The alternative, which currently enjoys more support, suggests that the Spartan agora was situated to the north of the Roman portico still within the Late Roman fortifications.

The Sanctuary of Artemis Orthia.

The Sanctuary of Artemis Orthia

The place named Limnaeum (Marshy) is sacred to Artemis Orthia (Upright). (3.16.7)

One of the best preserved complexes in ancient Sparta is the Sanctuary of Artemis Orthia. The sanctuary lies to the north-east of the centre of the modern day city, on the right bank of the river Eurotas. The earliest traces of a cult in this place date to the end of the 8th century BCE. A small temple was erected at this time with measurements of around 4.5 by 12.5 metres, as well as an altar dedicated to the goddess. Around 570 BCE, the complex was completely rebuilt, perhaps as the result of destruction caused by a flood. At this time, the sanctuary was enlarged, the altar was renovated and the temple was rebuilt. The new Doric building was made entirely of limestone and had measurements of around 7.5 by 16.75 metres.

Today, the foundations of a small, Doric temple bereft of columns from the 2nd century BCE can be seen on the excavation site (standing on the site of the earlier, Archaic temple), as well as a low, Roman altar (also standing on the site of its predecessor from the 6th century BCE). Around it, traces of the stands of an amphitheatre dating to the 3rd century CE can be discerned. It was erected for members of the public wishing to observe the annual, sanguineous contests which honoured the goddess. In these competitions, young Spartans were often flogged so hard that their blood gushed out onto the altar.

The remains of the temple in the Sanctuary of Artemis Orthia.

Menelaion

The name of Therapne is derived from the daughter of Lelex, and in it is a temple of Menelaus; they say that Menelaus and Helen were buried here. (Pausanias: 3.19.9)

Menalaion is a small archaeological site situated several kilometres to the south of Sparta. Many researchers believe that it is was the base of the mythical king, Menelaus, the husband of the beautiful Helen, who was the cause of the Trojan War. The name of the site comes from the remains of a sanctuary at the peak of its elevation dedicated to Menelaus and Helen. The site is also worth visiting for its breathtaking views of both the valley of the river Eurotas and the colossal Taygetus mountain range that rises to its west.

The construction visible today on this hill was initially identified in the 19th century as Therapne, a place mentioned by Pausanias in his journal. Heinrich Schliemann dug here in search of the Palace of Menelaus, but was not rewarded for his efforts. It was only in 1909 that archaeologists from the British Archaeological School of Athens came across the remains of a Mycenaean building during excavation work. Excavations were begun anew by the British in 1973 and continued thereafter for four consecutive seasons.

Menelaion was first inhabited at the end of the Neolithic period. In the Early Bronze Age, a small settlement existed here which then expanded in the Middle Helladic period to such an extent that it covered an area of one kilometre in length running across the whole of the elevation. In the 15th century BCE, an extensive building (Mansion 1) was constructed, probably for the local leader or perhaps for use as an administrative centre.

View towards the Shrine of Menelaus and Helen.

The Early Mycenaean Mansion 1 was built on a natural terrace in the eastern part of the site. It consisted of three complexes divided by corridors, which created a layout that was later echoed in the famous Palace of Nestor in Pylos. Indeed, the main building of Mansion 1 had exactly the same design as the throne room in Pylos, as it contained an entrance portico, a lobby, and a main room. Some researchers now believe that similar Early

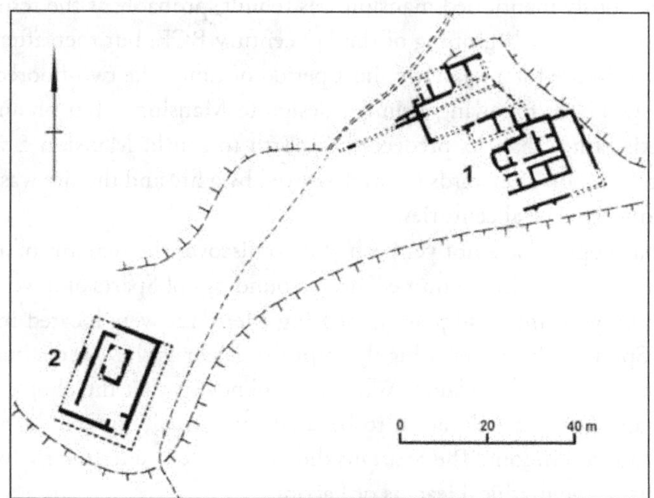

Plan of Menelaion: 1 – Mansion 2, 2 – Shrine of Menelaus and Helen (after Catling 1976–1977, Fig. 2).

Menelaion. The remains of Mycenaean buildings.

Mycenaean architectural complexes existed in centres such as Mycenae, Tiryns and Pylos. However, they would have been completely destroyed during the construction of palaces in the 14th century BCE.

Menelaion was one of the most important Late Helladic sites in Laconia. The previously mentioned mansion was rebuilt, probably as the result of an earthquake, at the beginning of the 14th century BCE, but thereafter it only remained in use for a relatively short period of time. The two-floored 'Mansion 2' was built following a similar design to Mansion 1, but on an east to west axis rather than its predecessor's north to south. Mansion 2 was also rebuilt, but soon afterwards it was destroyed by a fire and the site was forgotten about for several centuries.

Archaeologists have not yet been able to discover the remains of a typical Mycenaean citadel in the immediate surroundings of Sparta and we also still do not know if the headquarters of King Menelaus were located in Mycenaean Sparta (which seems highly improbable) or if they were situated on the site of today's Menelaion. What we do know is that the choice of both their patron and the elevation to be used for his cult site would not have been made at random. The Spartans did, after all, consider themselves to be the heirs of the mythical leaders of Laconia.

At first, in the 8th century BCE, only an altar was constructed on the Menelaion site, but by the end of the 7th or the beginning of the 6th century

The Shrine of Menelaus and Helen.

BCE, a small shrine built of limestone had joined it. The platform which we can now see, which must once have been at least five metres high, was added in the 5th century BCE and some researchers believe that it commemorated victory over the Persians. A ramp ran up its western side that would have been the path taken by animals which were to be sacrificed.

The structure we can see on top of the platform is not very well preserved, but it may have been an altar or a small shrine containing statues of Menelaus and Helen. The existence of a cult of this mythical, royal couple has been confirmed up until Roman times by archaeologists.

PRACTICAL INFORMATION:

Modern Sparta has little in common with its ancient predecessor and most tourists steer well clear of it, unless it is used as a stopping off point on the way to nearby Mystras, a town full of Byzantine and medieval monasteries.

Those seeking traces of the legendary Menelaus (the husband of the beautiful Helen) head for Menelaion, which lies several kilometres to the south of Sparta. Those hoping to see something commemorating Leonidas, however, will have to be satisfied with a modern monument dedicated to the great king of Sparta.

If you do choose to stop in Sparta, it is worth visiting the archaeological museum in the city centre. It is in slight disrepair, but it possesses several interest-

ing objects connected to the ancient history of the city. You should definitely see the marble bust of a hoplite (commonly known as Leonidas) and several portrait heads of Roman emperors (including one of the young Tiberius) are also worthy of your attention. A small, bronze statue of the 'Beautiful Helen', discovered during excavations at nearby Menelaion, can also be sought out amongst the other exhibits in one of the display cabinets.

After visiting the museum, it is possible to visit a park located in the northern part of the city that wraps around the former acropolis of Sparta. Whilst walking along the paths, which pass through olive groves, it is possible to discern the remains of the city walls, the agora and the building mentioned by Pausanias known as the Persian portico or Circular Building.

On the northern slope of the acropolis, the remains of a Roman theatre have been preserved and at the very peak are the foundations of two temples dedicated to Athena, as well as the ruins of a Byzantine church.

The bust of a hoplite (Leonidas).

Aside from the acropolis, the only other place in Sparta with preserved ancient remains is the Sanctuary of Artemis Orthia, which is situated in the north-eastern part of the town. It is hard to reach, but if you manage it you will be able to see the remains of a small temple, an altar and a viewing gallery, where people would once have sat to witness sanguineous rituals in honour of the gods.

Unfortunately, that is all that remains of the once mighty Sparta. The city will undoubtedly prove a disappointment to lovers of Greek art and architecture, but at least you can console yourself with the thought that you have trodden upon the same turf as Leonidas did so many years ago with his 300 heroic warriors.

Sparta can be reached by car without difficulty and buses run frequently to Athens and Kalamata (from where you can continue to Athens by train), as well as other destinations. If arriving by bus, all of the sights of note can be easily visited within a time frame of around three or four hours. In a car, nearby Menelaion (with beautiful views of Sparta and Mount Taygetus) lies within reach, as does the previously mentioned Mystras. In Sparta itself, there may be issues with parking in the centre (for access to the museum), but there are many free spaces around the acropolis.

Tourists in possession of an automobile should most definitely take the narrow, winding road through the Taygetus Mountains to Kalamata. Breathtaking views are guaranteed.

Archaeological Museum of Sparta:
Open:
Monday-Sunday: 8 a.m. – 3 p.m.
Tickets: *Full – 2 Euros; Reduced – 1 Euro*
Special ticket package valid for: Archaeological Museum of Sparta, Archaeological Museum of Mystras, Monemvasia Archaeological Collection, Museum of Pikoulakis Tower-House, Archaeological Site of Mystras: Full – 2 Euros; Reduced – 1 Euro
Free admission days: *6 March, 18 April, 18 May, 5 June, 27 September, the last weekend of September, Sundays in the period between 1 November and 31 March, National Holidays*
Museum closed: *1 January, 25 March, Easter Sunday, 1 May, 25–26 December*

It should be remembered that many people (from member states of the European Union) are entitled to free entry to the archaeological sites of Greece. This includes those over 65 or under 18, students and academic instructors.

It is always worth checking at the entrance about the possibility of a discount to the ticket price. A website prepared by the Greek Ministry of Tourism is also of assistance in this matter: http://odysseus.culture.gr/index_en.html

Acropolis of Sparta:
Open-air site. Permanently open.

Sanctuary of Artemis Orthia:
The archaeological site is not accessible to the public due to restoration work.

Menelaion:
Open-air site. Permanently open.

Doric columns of the Temple of Hera.

OLYMPIA

By the time you reach Olympia the Alpheius is a large and very pleasant river to see, ... (Pausanias: 5.7.1)

Olympia is located in the north-western Peloponnese on the right bank of the river Alpheios at the foot of the Hill of Kronos. It was one of the most important cult places for all Greeks and a sanctuary dedicated to Zeus, the most important god of the Greek pantheon, was found here.

According to Pausanias, it was in Olympia that the little Zeus was tended to by five Cretan brothers from Mount Ida, the oldest of whom was Heracles. This was not, however, the Heracles (the son of Zeus) famed for the twelve labours which he completed for Eurystheus of Tiryns, but one who had lived several generations earlier known as Heracles of Ida. According to another legend, Olympia was the place where Zeus the Thunderer challenged his father, Kronos, to a fistfight, as a result of which he took control of the entire world.

Archaeologists date the beginnings of Olympia to the Early Bronze Age. Over the course of excavations carried out here, remains of rectangular houses with apses (made of unworked rock and sun dried bricks) have been discovered from this period. A cemetery of chamber tombs from the times of the Mycenaean civilisation (Late Bronze Age) has also been discovered in the surrounding area. The question remains, however, as to whether the place was already a cult place of significance in this period.

The Greek writer Strabo, who lived in the 1st century BCE, stated that Olympia owed its renown to the local oracle, who specialised in military affairs. Two ancient local families of soothsayers are said to have lived here: the Lamides and the Clytiads. However, this has thus far been impossible to confirm.

Bronze and clay figurines discovered by archaeologists have been dated to the 11th to 9th centuries BCE, whilst discovered traces of the making of offerings suggests that the site of Olympia was already a cult place at this time. Amongst the finds, various types of votive gifts dominate. These include numerous figurines of horses, which implies the important role of the breeding of this animal in the western part of the Peloponnese, as well as its significance to the early cult of Zeus

Within the Altis there is also a sacred enclosure consecrated to Pelops, ... (Pausanias: 5.13.1)

The remains of Early Helladic houses (in the foreground) and the Hill of Kronos (in the background).

From the early period of development of the sanctuary (10th century BCE) comes the Pelopion, which was located in its central part and was both a cult place and the grave of Pelops, the main hero of Elis. Pelops is supposed to have come to the Peloponnese from Lydia in Asia Minor. When he discovered that Oenomaus, the king of Pisa in Elis, would give his beautiful daughter to anybody who could defeat him in a chariot race, he decided to take up the challenge. He did this in the full knowledge that around fifteen other daring characters had already forfeited their lives in their failed attempts, as Oenomaus had the right to kill anybody who he beat in the race. Oenomaus' chariot was harnessed to horses that were quicker than the wind, which were given to him by Ares, the god of war. As there seemed no way to defeat him, Pelops paid the charioteer of Oenomaus, Myrtilos, to sabotage the royal chariot. During the race, the chariot fell apart and the king lost his life, as had been predicted by an oracle who said his son-in-law would one day kill him. Pelops married the beautiful Hippodamia and acceded to the throne of Pisa. Olympia soon also fell under his control.

The Pelopion was surrounded by a protective earth mound of about thirty metres in diameter. It was constructed on top of prehistoric remains of Early Helladic houses and the ritual tumulus believed to have been of the hero himself. In the 6th century BCE, the site was rebuilt giving it the shape of an irregular polygon, before a monumental propylon was added in the 5th century BCE. In the centre of the Pelopion stood an altar and a statue of Pelops.

Heracles, … matched his brothers, as a game, in a running-race, and crowned the winner with a branch of wild olive, … (Pausanias: 5.7.7)

Olympia is known above all for the pan-Hellenic 'Olympic Games' that took place here, the founder of which is supposed to have been the Heracles of Ida mentioned earlier. He was then succeeded as organiser by many others including Pelops, Augeas (the owner of the famous stables which Heracles had to clean) and finally Heracles himself, who defeated Augeas in revenge for being banished from Elis.

After King Oxylos took his turn to organise the Games, Pausanias states that there was a long break in their staging lasting many generations until the rule of a certain King Iphitos.

According to Greek historiography, the Games recommenced in 776 BCE and from then on took place every four years in summer between the 27th of July and the 27th of September. In their classical form, the Games lasted five days and only Greeks were allowed to participate. They competed against each other in sporting contests such as running, pentathlon (run, long jump, discus, javelin and wrestling), boxing, pankration and chariot racing. The winners, or 'olimpionikai' as they were named, were awarded with a modest wreath of olive branches brought from the land of the Hyperboreans and planted, according to legend, by Heracles of Ida on the grounds of the sanctuary. An additional prize was the right to place a statue in Olympia commemorating the victory.

The Games also made Olympia an important political centre. Treaties signed between different lands were often put on display to the public here

The Stadium. View from the North-East.

and Greek poleis competed against each other by erecting treasuries and other buildings to mark their military successes.

In the 6th century BCE, the citizens of Elis (which lay forty kilometres to the north-west of Olympia) took control of both the sanctuary and the Games themselves. This did not, however, prevent Olympia from becoming one of the most impressive architectural sites of Greece on a par with both Delphi and Athens.

In 338 BCE, Philip II of Macedon was honoured by being granted permission to construct the 'Philippeion' within the sanctuary. This building showed the imperial aspirations of his family and sanctioned Macedonian rule over all of Greece.

In the Hellenistic period, Olympia remained in full bloom and its prosperity continued up until the early period of Roman rule in Greece. It came to an end in 86 BCE, when General Sulla plundered the sanctuary and took the majority of its treasures back to Rome.

Roman patronage in the period of Imperial Rome, however, contributed to the regeneration of the sanctuary and the Olympic Games and the Statue of Zeus created by Phidias (one of the seven wonders of the ancient world) became powerful symbols uniting the Greeks under Roman rule.

Even the Romans appreciated the importance of the Olympian sanctuary. Marcus Vipsanius Agrippa (the son-in-law of Emperor Augustus) carried

The Sanctuary of Zeus. The Hill of Kronos in the background.

out repairs to the Temple of Zeus after it was damaged by a powerful earthquake in 40 BCE, Emperor Tiberius won the chariot race here in 4 BCE and Emperor Nero (who took part in musical contests which were specially organised for him in 67 CE) was one of the biggest donors to the sanctuary.

When Pausanias was travelling across Greece in the 2nd century CE, Olympia was still the location where the most important sporting events of the ancient world took place. During the final development of the sanctuary, which took place during precisely this period, new baths and a modern system of water supply to the buildings were created. This whole project was financed by Herodes Atticus.

In the second half of the 3rd century CE, as a result of the military threat of barbarian invasion from the north (by the Heruli amongst others), the decision was taken to build a defensive wall around the temple. It was created using material from numerous buildings which had already been destroyed. The Temple of Zeus was restored for the final time in around 300 CE but the Games continued to be held until at least the second half of the 4th century CE. This has been attested by the discovery of an inscription by archaeologists which named two Athenian brothers the victors during the games of 381 and 385 CE. At the beginning of the 5th century CE, the 'workshop' of Phidias was converted into a church for the local Christian community, whose houses and workshops were located in the vicinity of the former sanctuary. In the 6th century CE, Olympia suffered both a flood and two powerful earthquakes which laid ruin to the majority of its buildings.

The hunt for 'treasures' hidden under the thick layer of sludge at the Olympia site began in the 18th century. Many tried unsuccessfully to obtain permission to excavate, including both French researchers and the famous German scholar of antiquity, Johann Winckelmann. Regular excavation work only began on the sanctuary in the 19th century and was initially carried out by French archaeologists. In 1875, the German Archaeological Institute took over the excavation site and worked here until 1881. Further research was then carried out mainly between the years 1936 to 1941 and 1951 to 1965. In these periods, the majority of the buildings of the sanctuary which have come to be so admired were uncovered. The work of the German Archaeological Institute at Olympia is still ongoing and its finds are exhibited in the wonderful and highly recommended archaeological museum that is situated at the entrance to the Sanctuary of Zeus. It is certainly worth visiting to witness the marvellous objects they have discovered within the sanctuary and its surroundings. The most important of these are a marble statue of Hermes and the Infant Dionysus by the famous sculptor Praxiteles, a marble statue of Nike chiselled by Paeonius, a bronze helmet given by Militiades as an offering after his victorious battle against the Persians and the extremely beautiful marble architectonic decoration of the Temple of Zeus.

The Site

A visit to the Sanctuary of Zeus begins in the northern section of the gymnasium, from whence a wide avenue leads to the south towards the heart of the Olympian sanctuary, known as 'Altis'.

The Town Hall of the Eleans is within the Altis, and it has been built beside the exit beyond the gymnasium. In this gymnasium are the running-tracks and the wrestling-grounds for the athletes. (Pausanias: 5.15.8)

It is precisely here, in the south-western part of the Sanctuary of Zeus, that the buildings designed for the use of athletes coming to Olympia were located. Of these buildings, the gymnasium was located the furthest to the north (visible to the right). It was originally an open space which was dedi-

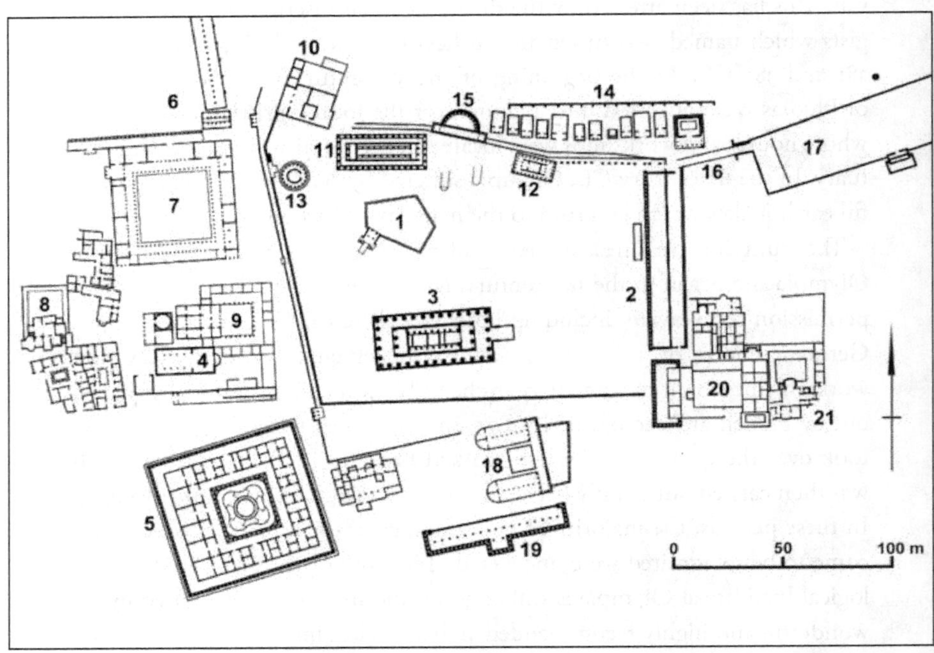

Plan of Olympia: 1 – Precinct of Pelops, 2 – Echo Stoa, 3 – Temple of Zeus, 4 – Workshop of Phidias, 5 – Leonidaion, 6 – Gymnasium, 7 – Palaestra, 8 – Baths, 9 – Courtyard Houses, 10 – Prytaneion, 11 – Temple of Hera, 12 – Metroon, 13 – Philippeion, 14 – Treasuries, 15 – Nymphaeum, 16 – Tunnel (secret entrance), 17 – Stadium, 18 – Bouleuterion, 19 – South Stoa, 20 – "Nero House", 21 – Roman Baths (after Kaltsas 2004, fig. 14).

The south part of the xystos in the Gymnasium.

cated to athletic training. With time, however, it became a regular architectural complex.

The remains of a large, nearly rectangular courtyard (of approximately 120 by 220 metres) surrounded by four Doric porticos have survived to our times. A xystos that contained two parallel running tracks (from the 2nd century CE) extended to its east. Opposite, on the west side (behind the portico), were once rooms which served as dormitories for the athletes, although

The western part of the Palaestra.

The north portico of the Palaestra.

this part of the gymnasium was unfortunately destroyed by the waters of the river Kladeos. A monumental Corinthian gate was built in the first half of the 2nd century BCE in the southern portico of the gymnasium and this led to the palaestra, which can be seen shortly to our right.

The palaestra (built in the 3rd century BCE) consisted of a courtyard with sides of around 66 metres surrounded by Doric porticos, behind which numerous rooms were located. One of these was the canteen (in the south-west corner), whilst two rooms to the north functioned as libraries and reading rooms. To the south-west of the palaestra, athletes were able to make use of baths. This part of the complex was built as early as the 5th century BCE and comprised the baths themselves, as well as an open swimming pool with measurements of 16 by 24 metres.

To the east (left) of the avenue proceeding towards Altis, not far from the south-east corner of the gymnasium, we can see the remains of the Prytaneion. According to Pausanias, this contained a sacred hearth and a dining room in which the residents of Elis feasted with the Olympic victors. The date of construction of the Prytaneion has not been conclusively established, although it should probably be dated to the end of the 1st century CE rather than to the 5th century BCE, as was previously supposed.

Between the Prytaneion and the gymnasium, there was once a gate that led from the north to the sacred precinct (Altis) of the Sanctuary of Zeus.

The sacred grove of Zeus has been called from of old Altis, a corruption of the word "alsos," which means a grove. (Pausanias: 5.10.1)

Altis, 'the sacred precinct', was the heart of the Olympian sanctuary. Its northern side lay against the Hill of Kronos and it was bordered to its south and west by a wall. To the east was the 97.81-metre long Doric portico of the nymph, Echo. At the time of Pausanias' visit, numerous statues of donors and victors in the games stood within Altis. Their bases have been preserved in situ in most cases.

The Metroum is within the Altis, and so is a round building called the Philippeum. (Pausanias: 5.20.9)

On entering the area of what was once Altis, we can see the remains of the partly reconstructed Philippeion to the left (east). It was a tholos constructed in the north-west corner of Altis and was funded by the Macedonian king, Philip II, after his victorious battle at Chaeronea (338 BCE). This round Ionic building (with a diameter of 15.24 metres) was made of local limestone and marble. The interior of the tholos contained statues of Philip and his family (including his wife, Olympias, and son, Alexander, who would later become Alexander the Great) made of gold and ivory and sculpted by the famous Leochares.

The Philippeion.

It remains after this for me to describe the temple of Hera ... The style of the temple is Doric, and pillars stand all round it. (Pausanias: 5.16.1)

Among the preserved Archaic remains of the sanctuary, some of the oldest belong to the Temple of Hera (the Heraion), which was located in the northern part of

The Temple of Hera. View from the East.

Altis, just next to the tholos of Philip II. The original Heraion I (from the first half of the 7th century BCE) was a hecatompedon, did not possess a peristasis and probably consisted of three parts: a pronaos, a cella and a small opisthodomos. The cella was divided into a nave and two aisles by two series of wooden columns within its interior. The later Heraion II was built on the site of the original Temple of Hera in around 600 BCE. It was initially a cult place of Zeus and Hera and only after the construction of the newer

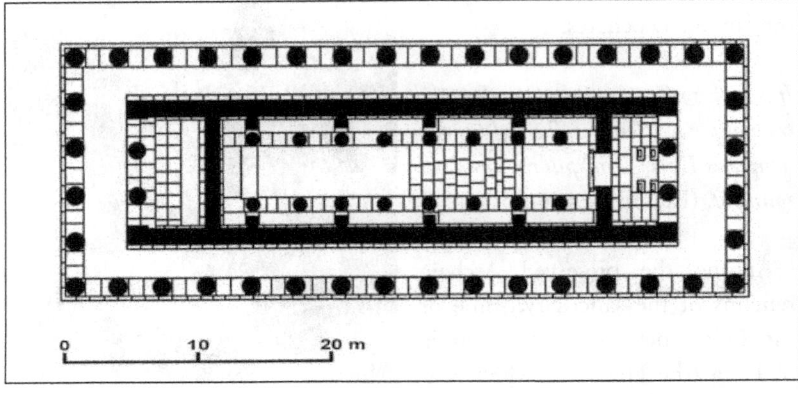

Plan of the Temple of Hera (after Dinsmoor 1975, fig. 19).

Temple of Zeus was it solely dedicated to Hera. It was a Doric peripteros (six by sixteen columns) with a cella, pronaos and opisthodomos. The columns were placed on a two-level crepidoma made of poros blocks. The stylobate was an extended rectangle with sides of 18.75 by 50 metres. The temple originally had wooden columns in the peristasis, which were gradually replaced by those made of stone. These were of varying sizes and included both shafts and capitals. The temple's gabled roof was covered with terracotta tiles and a terracotta acroterion was placed on its top.

When Pausanias visited the Temple of Hera, it was simply performing the function of a 'museum' filled with valuable objects. These included around twenty gold and ivory statues (including Hera, Zeus, Athena, Demeter, Apollo and Artemis), as well as one of the marvels of Olympia, the Chest of Cypselus. The chest was made of cedar wood, probably at the beginning of the 6th century BCE, and masterful application was evident in its figures made of gold, wood and ivory.

The previously mentioned marble statue of Hermes and the Infant Dionysus, probably the work of the famous sculptor, Praxiteles, was also positioned in the Heraiaon in the times of Pausanias, where it was later discovered by German researchers. It is now the greatest source of pride of the archaeological museum of Olympia.

To the east of the Temple of Hera, the remains of a once impressive nymphaeum (monumental fountain) dating to around 153 CE can be seen. Both the fountain and the aqueduct which supplied it with water were built using funds provided by the renowned Herodes Atticus in honour of his wife, Regilla. The water supplied by the aqueduct flowed into the upper basin.

The Nymphaeum of Herodes Atticus.

From here it passed through nozzles in the form of lion heads to the lower rectangular basin lying below, which was flanked by round colonnades (*monopteroi* in Greek). The back wall contained apses and niches containing a total of 24 statues presenting Herodes and members of his family in the upper part and the imperial family below. The whole construction was laid out in beautiful coloured marble. The nymphaeum built by Herodes Atticus replaced a saltwater well located on the same site that had been one of Olympia's claims to fame in antiquity.

A temple of no great size in the Doric style they have called down to the present day Metroum, ... (Pausanias: 5.20.9)

In the 4th century BCE, a great deal of building work took place within the sanctuary, which included the construction of the 'Metroon', the remains of which can be seen when continuing further east from the Temple of Hera. The Metroon, a sanctuary dedicated to the mother goddess known also as Rhea (the mother of Zeus), was a small, Doric, peripteral temple with six by eleven columns and measurements of 10.62 by 20.67 metres. In the times of Emperor Augustus, the temple site was greatly developed, leading to the citizens of Elis' decision to dedicate it to the first Roman emperor. This is described in an inscription in the architrave which dedicates the construction to the 'Saviour of the Greeks and the entire populated world'. From

The Metroon. View from the East.

this time onwards, the building began to perform the role of a cult place of deified Roman emperors.

When investigating the temple, German archaeologists discovered eight statues of emperors which were once positioned inside it, a fact which was also mentioned by Pausanias. They are all now to be found in the local museum, with the exception of one, which is exhibited in Berlin.

There is in the Altis to the north of the Heraeum a terrace of conglomerate, and behind it stretches Mount Cronius. On this terrace are the treasuries, ... (Pausanias: 6.19.1)

Above the Metroon, we can now turn our attention to a broad terrace located at the very foot of the Hill of Kronos, on which eleven treasuries were built between the years 560 to 450 BCE. These buildings, which resembled little temples, were constructed by Greek poleis to hold the gifts which they were to offer. The first to be built was the treasury of the Sicilian city of Gela (560 BCE) and it is situated furthest east. Further west are the remains of the treasuries of: Megara (around 510 BCE), Metapontum, Selinunte, two treasuries of Cyrene, Sybaris (before 510 BCE), Byzantion, Epidamnos (around 525 BCE), Syracuse (the beginning of the 5th century BCE) and Sicyon (around 450 BCE). In the times of Pausanias, the treasuries were used to store various valuable objects, such as the gold-hilted 'Sword of Pelops'

The Treasuries at the foot of the Hill of Kronos.

The Tunnel (secret entrance) leading to the Stadium.

and the ivory 'Horn of Amalthea' (Pausanias: 6.19.6), which he was able to admire in the Treasury of the Sicyonians.

Continuing east from the Metroon, we come after a while to the ruins of the previously mentioned Doric portico of the nymph, Echo, to our right. It was constructed around halfway through the 4th century BCE and it was later totally rebuilt, probably during the reign of Emperor Augustus. The name of the portico was given ... *because when a man has shouted his voice it is repeated by the echo seven or even more times* (Pausanias: 5.21.17). The Echo Portico replaced an earth tribune which had been previously used by those participating in ritual ceremonies taking place in Altis.

In front of the portico, the remains of the largest honorific monument standing within the Altis precinct can be seen. It was an oblong platform of about twenty metres in length that once supported a pair of Ionic marble columns. These were about nine metres high and topped by statues. Two inscriptions discovered by archaeologists inform us that these statues were of the leader of Hellenistic Egypt, Ptolemy II (282–246 BCE), and his sister-wife, Arsinoe II.

At the end of the statues which they made from the fines levied on athletes, there is the entrance called the Hidden Entrance. Through it umpires and competitors are wont to enter the stadium. Now the stadium is an embankment of earth, ... (Pausanias: 6.20.8)

Just to the north of the Echo Portico are the remains of a building which Pausanias called the secret entrance to the stadium. It was built around 200 BCE and took the form of a curved tunnel leading into the stadium, which was used by officials (*hellanodikai* in Greek) and competitors. It was fronted by an arched gateway which has been partially restored in modern times. In front of the gate now stand a row of bases intended for bronze statues of Zeus termed 'Zanes' (the plural form of Zeus). The statues were financed by fines paid by athletes who broke Olympic rules, mainly by offering bribes to the officials or paying off opponents. Pausanias mentioned seeing fourteen such statues during his visit to Olympia, which had been built from 388 BCE onwards.

After passing through the small, curved tunnel, we now find ourselves standing in the famous Olympic stadium. The stadium which can currently be seen was built in the 4th century BCE as an enlarged version of its predecessor, which was located on the same site. It could hold 40,000 spectators seated directly on earth embankments. The running track was 191.78 metres long and was intended for twenty runners. In its southern section, we can see the place where the officials would have stood, which is a surprisingly distant sixty metres from the start/finish line. In the northern section opposite is a stone altar to the goddess, Demeter Chamyne. The priestess of this goddess was allowed to watch the events from here, the only female who was allowed onto the stadium's premises.

After visiting the stadium, returning down the curved tunnel and turning to the south (left), we pass the Echo Portico and move in the direction of

The seats of the officials (hellanodikai) in the Stadium.

the southern part of Altis, where the remains of one of the most marvellous Greek temples once stood, the Temple of Olympian Zeus.

The temple and the image were made for Zeus from spoils, ... The temple is in the Doric style, and the outside has columns all around it. (Pausanias: 5.10.2)

The monumental Temple of Zeus in Olympia was built between the years 470 to 456 BCE and its creator was the local architect, Libon of Elis. The temple and the statue found within it were gifts of gratitude, paid for by the inhabitants of the city of Elis with war spoils from their victories against their eternal rivals, the citizens of Pisa.

It was a Doric peripteros (six by thirteen columns) made of local limestone and then covered in coloured stucco. A ramp on its eastern side led up to the platform on which the temple was built. The stylobate of the temple had measurements of 27.68 by 64.12 metres and its interior consisted of a nave with two aisles in the cella, as well as a small pronaos and an opisthodomos that was also used as a meeting room.

The surviving monumental sculptural decoration of the Temple of Zeus, which can be seen in the archaeological museum next to the site, is an excellent example of Early Classical architectonic design. The preserved sculptures of the eastern gable depict the mythical beginnings of the Olympic Games,

The Temple of Zeus. View from the East.

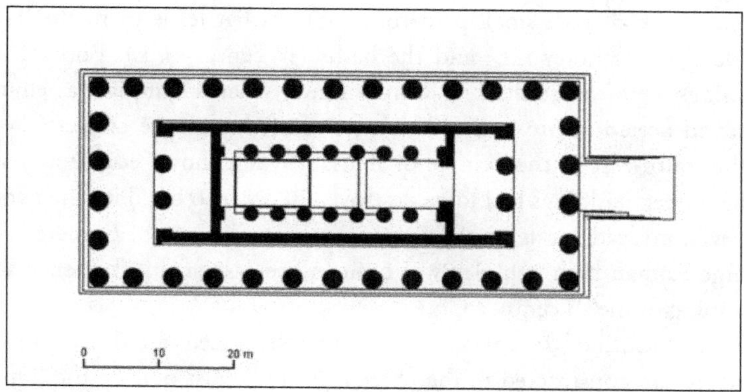

Plan of the Temple of Zeus (after Dinsmoor 1975, fig. 55).

namely the preparations for the chariot race between Pelops and Oenomaus, which a standing Zeus watches over from the centre of the image. The sculptures of the western gable show the fight between the Lapiths and the centaurs in the presence of Apollo. In addition, twelve metopes presenting the Labours of Heracles have also survived to the present day.

The god sits on a throne, and he is made of gold and ivory. (Pausanias: 5.11.1)

Inside the cella stood the chryselephantine Statue of Zeus by Phidias, considered to be one of the seven wonders of the ancient world. Zeus was seated on a richly decorated throne, adorned with gold figures which included sphinxes. Nike stood on his right hand and in his left he wielded a sceptre which was crowned by a gold eagle. Access to the statue was restricted by a marble barrier, but those who wished to better view the figure of the august god could make use of a viewing gallery on the first floor of the temple.

The Temple of Zeus was repaired several times in antiquity after earthquakes, a phenomenon that plagued the area. It was probably already bereft of its roof when a massive earthquake destroyed its peristasis in the 6th century CE. The Statue of Zeus had earlier been moved to Constantinople in around 395 CE, but it was later to burn there in the great fire of 475 CE.

To the north of the temple stood the eschara altar of Zeus, where sacrifices were made to the god. The mountain of ash, created in part by the constantly burning sacred fire of the Prytaneion (which was ritually mixed with the waters of the River Alpheios), reached a height of seven metres in the 2nd century CE.

To the south-east of the Temple of Zeus are the remains of several buildings which were not mentioned by Pausanias. Opposite the entrance to the temple, we can see a small path running east that leads us to the 'House of Nero' (2nd century CE) and the baths (3rd century CE). Both of these buildings were constructed in Roman times, when Olympia was enjoying a second period of prosperity. The remains of the 'House of Nero' lie just to the south-east of the Temple of Zeus. It was a showy edifice and some earlier Greek buildings had to be destroyed in order to build it. The name is, however, misleading, as it was constructed after the rule of Emperor Nero. A large Roman bath complex was built to the east of this residence at the beginning of the 3rd century CE.

Directly south of the entrance to the Temple of Zeus are the remains of a bouleuterion constructed in the 6th century BCE just outside the limits of Altis. In Roman times, it was the seat of the 'Olympic Committee', an Elean body which administered the games and the sanctuary. It was also the place where participants swore to obey the rules of fair play. It was an unusual building, since it consisted of two rooms finished with apses which were constructed at different times. The older one (to the north) was built around 550 BCE, whilst the newer was constructed around 500 BCE. Later on (around 370 BCE), an additional large room was added on which connected the two previously existing ones. The completed whole was now fronted to the east by an Ionic portico, also constructed in the 4th century BCE.

To the south of the bouleuterion stood the South Stoa (erected around 350 BCE), which perhaps served as an observation point for distinguished guests. It faced south and therefore had a view of both the processional way and the hippodrome. The latter has not as yet been researched by archaeologists.

The Bouleuterion. View from the North.

The Leonidaion.

Moving to the west, we come after a short while to the massive, rectangular construction called the 'Leonidaion'.

The Leonidaeum is outside the sacred enclosure, but at the processional entrance to the Altis, ... (Pausanias: 5.15.2)

The Leonidaion is located in the south-western part of the sanctuary. It was built over an area of 6,000 square metres around 350 BCE, when it became the largest building of Olympia. It was a gift of Leonidas, son of Leotes, from Naxos. This is attested by inscriptions discovered by archaeologists on the architraves of both sides of the building. Surrounded by an Ionic portico and containing rooms situated around a columned courtyard, the building would have acted as a sort of hotel and a place where banquets would have been held, above all by the aristocracy visiting Olympia for the horse races.

Around halfway through the 2nd century CE, the Leonidaion was used as an occasional residence of the Roman Prefect of Greece following its reconstruction after a fire. Its internal courtyard was transformed into an irrigated garden with a centrally located island reminiscent of the garden of the marvellous imperial villa of Emperor Hadrian in Tibur (modern day Tivoli) on the outskirts of Rome.

Outside the Altis there is a building called the workshop of Pheidias, ... In the building is an altar to all the gods in common. (Pausanias: 5.15.1)

Walking along the southern and then (turning right) western edges of the Leonidaion, we soon come to a building which Pausanias described as the 'workshop of Phidias'. It was the second highest building of the sanctuary after the Temple of Zeus and was designed for work on the over twelve-metre high Statue of Zeus. Its interior was reminiscent of the cella of the temple to which the statue was subsequently moved. According to Pausanias, the former workshop of Phidias contained an altar dedicated to all the gods when he visited in the 2nd century CE. Later, in the 5th century CE, the complex was transformed into a church, the interior of which was laid out in marble. During research conducted here, archaeologists discovered the two latest inscriptions of ancient Olympia, which mention priests called Kyriakos and Andreas.

The Workshop of Phidias.

Before what is called Theëcoleon is a building, in a corner of which has been set up an altar of Pan. (Pausanias: 5.15.8)

Directly to the north of Phidias' workshop (between it and the palaestra which we have already visited), the remains of two 'houses' with columned courtyards can be seen, although it is uncertain what their exact functions were. The earlier of them dates to around 450 BCE and was probably an older palaestra and not (as is usually supposed) a house of priests (Theëcoleon). In the 1st century BCE, the complex was partially destroyed in order to make room for a second, considerably larger 'house'. It is probably this building that was intended for workers serving in the sanctuary, including priests.

To the north of the 'house of priests' is the palaestra and Philippeion mentioned at the beginning of this guide. From here, we return down the avenue to the main entrance, where we conclude our visit to Olympia.

PRACTICAL INFORMATION:

The archaeological site of Olympia lies in the western part of the Peloponnese, around fifteen kilometres to the east of the city of Pyrgos. The complex is situated at the foot of the Hill of Kronos on an enchanting plain at the confluence of the Alpheios and Kladeos rivers. It developed continuously from Mycenaean times up to the Byzantine period and the buildings which we can now admire therefore come from all the different stages of development of Greek civilisation.

Olympia is unquestionably a place that should be included on the route of every tourist travelling across Greece. It is a wonderfully pleasant site both to visit and to walk around, as it is situated on a broad plain containing many trees and shrubs that offer shade on hot, sunny days.

Olympia is relatively easy to reach by car. The journey from Athens (at least 260km) takes around three to four hours, whereas from Patras (120km) it is under two. It can also be reached directly by bus from Patras. There is no bus service between Athens and Olympia, but it is possible to first travel to Pyrgos (four hours) and then to switch to a local bus to take you to Olympia itself (30 minutes).

As it is quite far distant from other archaeological sites of interest within the Peloponnese, it is worth staying the night in Olympia. The modern town of Archaia Olympia is set up to cater for a huge amount of tourists, although most tend to arrive on organised excursions. Numerous hotels and eateries can thus be found of varying standard and price. Reservations can be made via Internet sites such as www.tripadvisor.com, www.booking.com or www.trivago.com.

The marble statue of Hermes and the infant Dionysus.

The archaeological site and museum are located in the southern part of town and a large car park is situated next to them.

Before beginning your visit to the site itself, you should have a look at the local archaeological museum. It contains probably the second richest collection of Greek art after the National Archaeological Museum of Athens. It is all presented in chronological order, beginning from prehistoric times and ending in the Byzantine period. Special attention should be paid to the marvellous architectural décor from the Temple of Zeus, the marble statue of Hermes and the Infant Dionysus (the work of the famous sculptor, Praxiteles), a marble statue of the goddess, Nike (chiselled by Paionios) and the bronze helmet given by Militiades as a votive offering after victory over the Persians in battle.

Following your visit to the museum, you can walk around the site itself, which should take between two to four hours, depending on your physical condition and the amount of time at your disposal. During your visit, you absolutely must see:

- *The Temple of Hera*
- *The Temple of Zeus*
- *The Tholos of Philip (II)*
- *The Workshop of Phidias*
- *The Olympic Stadium*

For those with more time, the following are also worth a visit:

- *The Palaestra*
- *The Gymnasium*
- *The Metroon*
- *The Nymphaeum of Herodes Atticus*
- *The Treasuries*
- *The Echo Portico*
- *The Leonidaion*

It is not possible to eat a meal or even purchase a drink on the site. You should therefore remember to take all necessary provisions with you (primarily water), especially if you plan on making a lengthy visit.

The marble statue of Apollo from the temple of Zeus.

Archaeological Site and the Museum:
Open:
1 April – 31 October:
Monday-Sunday: 8 a.m. – 8 p.m.;
1 November – 31 March:
Monday-Friday: 8 a.m. – 5 p.m., Saturday-Sunday and National Holidays: 8 a.m. – 3 p.m.
Tickets: *Full – 6 Euros; Reduced – 3 Euros*
Special ticket package valid for the archaeological site and the museum: Full – 9 Euros; Reduced – 5 Euros
Free admission days: *6 March, 18 April, 18 May, 5 June, the last weekend of September, every first Sunday from November 1st to March 31st*
Site closed: *1 January, 25 March, Easter Sunday, 1 May, 25–26 December*

It should be remembered that many people (from member states of the European Union) are entitled to free entry to the archaeological sites of Greece. This includes those over 65 or under 18, students and academic instructors.

It is always worth checking at the entrance about the possibility of a discount to the ticket price. A website prepared by the Greek Ministry of Tourism is also of assistance in this matter: http://odysseus.culture.gr/index_en.html

GLOSSARY

Abaton – A place within a sanctuary which may only be accessed by a select group of people, e.g. priests. In the Sanctuary of Asclepius in Epidaurus, the abaton was also used as an enkoimeterion.

Acanthus – A genus of herbaceous plants growing in the Mediterranean region and used as a decorative motif on Corinthian capitals.

Acroterion – In ancient architecture, a decorative element in the form of a figure, bas-relief or ornament which adorns an apex and/or the lower corners of a triangular gable of a temple or other building.

Adyton – The holiest part of a Greek temple which only priests may enter.

Aedicule – A niche framed by two columns or pilasters bearing an entablature and pediment.

Amphiprostyle – A type of Greek temple with a colonnade in its facade and also to its rear.

Amphora – A vessel, most often of an elongated shape, with two vertical handles. Most often used to store or transport liquids (wine and olive oil) and granular products.

Anta (pl. antae) – A pillar in a Greek temple which forms the end of a protruding side wall, thereby creating a vestibule.

Apodyterium – A room in Roman baths used for changing.

Apse – A semi-circular room or recess.

Architrave – In ancient architecture, the lowest part of the entablature. It lies directly atop the capitals of the columns and below a tryglyph-metope (Doric order) or continuous (Ionic and Corinthian orders) frieze.

Arcosolium – An arched niche carved into rock.

Aryballos (pl. aryballoi) – A small vessel designed to store oils used in the embrocation of bodies.

Atrium – An open courtyard surrounded by a colonnaded covered walkway. Found in Roman houses and in front of Byzantine churches, often with a cistern below it.

Attic – The storey above the main entablature, often containing dwarf pilasters, reliefs or inscriptions.

Betyl – A rectangular stele carved in a relief or in the form of a portable idol and often placed in a niche. In Aramaic, the word 'betyl' means 'house of god'. The Nabataeans used the betyl to represent deities.

Biclinium – A room with two benches designed for dining, sometimes as part of a funeral.

Bouleuterion – In ancient Greece, the seat of the city council (boule) and the place where they met.

Caldarium – A room in Roman baths which contained a pool of hot water.

Capital – The top element of the column or pilaster. It is often a form of decoration.

Caryatid – In the Ionic order, a support which has the appearance of a woman and is used to hold up the entablature of a building.

Cavea – The viewing area or auditorium in Roman theatres, most often semi-circular. The equivalent of the Greek 'theatron'.

Cella – In ancient architecture, the most important, central room of a temple, which normally contained a statue of the god to whom the temple was dedicated.

Cenotaph – A kind of symbolic grave dedicated to a person buried elsewhere.

Columbarium – A tomb with niches for urns containing ashes, sometimes used as a dovecote.

Cornice – In classical architecture, the upper element of an entablature above the architrave and frieze.

Crepidoma – In Greek architecture, a stone platform upon which a building (e.g. temple) was raised. It normally consisted of three levels; the two lower ones were termed the stereobate, whilst the upper was the stylobate.

Crowstep – Crenellations with stepped sides, used as decoration on Nabataean tombs.

Diazoma – A horizontal passage between sectors (kerkides) of the viewing area in a Greek theatre.

Distyle in antis – In ancient architecture, a small, rectangular temple with antae at the front and at the rear.

Doric frieze – A frieze of the Doric order decorated with alternating triglyphs and metopes.

Dromos – The long, narrow corridor in tholos tombs leading to the funerary chamber.

Dwarf pilaster – A small pilaster.

Enkoimeterion – A building within a sanctuary of Asclepius (normally a stoa) which was intended for the ritual dreaming of the infirm. During their slumber, they would be either cured of their ailment or would discover in which way they may be healed.

Entablature – In classical architecture, the horizontal structure above the capitals. It consists of an architrave, frieze and cornice.

Eschara – A type of altar upon which sacrifices offered to the gods were burnt. It sometimes took the form of a mound formed of burnt ashes.

Exedra – In ancient architecture, a semi-circular, open niche.

Fascia – A broad flat band used in classical architecture.

Flutes – Vertical grooves in the shaft of a column.

Frieze – The middle element of a classical entablature located between the architrave and cornice.

Frigidarium – A room in Roman baths which contained a cold pool.

Hecatompedon – A temple building of 100 feet in length (approximately 33 metres).

Herm – In ancient Greece, a four-sided post, sometimes topped by a bust or head of Hermes, which was placed by the side of the road at crossroads or in city squares.

Heroon – A place or building (most often a tomb or cenotaph) dedicated to a fallen hero.

Hestiatorion – A building or room used for dining.

Hexastyle – A building with six columns in its facade.

Hydria – A jug with a round mid-section, a high neck and three handles (two horizontal and one vertical) designed to carry water.

Hypocaust – The heating system in Roman baths. It blew hot air in from underneath the floor (which was supported by pillars).

Ionic frieze – A frieze of the Ionic order. It could be flat or decorated with ornaments or figural depictions.

In situ – In its original location.

Katagogeion – In ancient Greece, a type of hotel where it was possible to stay the night for a fee.

Kore – In Archaic Greek sculpture, a statue of a girl wearing clothes who is standing up.

Kouros – In Archaic Greek sculpture, a statue of a naked young man who is standing up.

Krater – A large vessel with two handles used to mix wine and water.

Lekythos – A vessel in the shape of a small jug used to store olive oil, scented oils or perfume. Lekythoi were also used in the cult of the dead as funerary gifts or as monuments placed on graves.

Lesche – In ancient Greece, a room or building intended for social gatherings.

Mausoleum – A monumental tomb, most often in the form of a freestanding, richly adorned building.

Megaron – A rectangular building with an entrance on its shortest side, consisting of a vestibule and one or two rooms in a line behind it. In Mycenaean palaces, the main room of the megaron contained a hearth surrounded by four columns used as ceiling support.

Metope – In the Doric order, a flat stone slab, sometimes covered with relief decoration, positioned between two tryglyphs.

Monopteros – A round building without walls comprising a circular colonnade supporting a conical roof.

Naos – A temple.

Narthex – In Early Christian architecture, a kind of transverse lobby fronting the entrance to a basilica.

Nave – A central space in church with two aisles, often separated by colonnades.

Nephesh – In Semitic languages, it means 'soul' and relates most frequently to commemorative stelae. In Nabataean art, it usually takes the form of a cone or obelisk standing on a rectangular or cylindrical base. The Nabataeans used the nephesh as a way to remember the dead.

Niche – A recess in a wall for a statue or other ornament, often rectangular or semicircular and sometimes arched.

Nymphaeum – In ancient Greece, it was initially a natural site (most often based around a spring) where nymphs were worshipped. In later times, however, it possessed architectural elements. In ancient Rome, it was a fountain (nymphaion), most often with monumental, architectonic framing, from which water (transported via pipes) emerged.

Odeon – A small theatre, sometimes roofed, where music or recitation contests were held.

Oinochoe – A vessel in the shape of a jug used to pour wine.

Oikos – In architecture, a small, rectangular room or building located within a sanctuary or city.

Octastyle – A building with eight columns in its façade.

Olpe – A vessel in the shape of an elongated jug used to pour wine.

Opisthodomos – In Greek temples, the rear room situated behind the cella.

Orchestra – A circular or semi-circular stage intended for the chorus in an ancient theatre.

Palaestra – A part of a gymnasium, most often taking the form a courtyard surrounded by porticos, which was used for training (wrestling, boxing).

Palmette – An ornament somewhat resembling a palm-leaf.

Pankration – In ancient Games, a brutal form of fighting which combined wrestling with boxing. Every hold and blow was allowed.

Parodos – In ancient theatres, the side passage between the viewing gallery and the stage leading to the orchestra. It was used by the public as an entrance to the theatre.

Paraskenion – In ancient theatres, side wings built onto the stage (proskenion) which were used as a way down to the orchestra.

Pastophorium – In early churches, two small rooms located on either side of the presbytery.

Pediment – In classical architecture, the structure crowning the front of the building. It often contains a sculpture in its tympanum.

Peribolos – A round, stone wall surrounding a tomb or tumulus.

Peripteros – A type of rectangular Greek temple, surrounded on all four sides by a colonnade (peristasis).

Peristasis – In ancient architecture, a colonnade surrounding a temple supporting an entablature.

Peristyle – In ancient architecture, a courtyard surrounded by a columned portico (colonnade).

Phiale – A vessel in the shape of a deep bowl used for drinking and cult rituals.

Pilaster – In ancient architecture, a flat pillar adjacent to a wall with a base and a capital, most often with a decorative rather than a constructive role.

Pithos – A large, clay vessel resembling a barrel used to store provisions (e.g. grain) and sometimes used in funerary rituals as a coffin.

Poliandron – In ancient Greece, a shared grave for warriors who fell in battle.

Polis – In ancient Greece, the political entity of a state. A city-state in the vernacular.

Praecinctio – In Roman theatres, a horizontal passageway between sectors (cuneus) of the viewing area. The equivalent of a Greek diazoma.

Pronaos – In Greek temples, the lobby in front of the cella.

Propylaea – In Greek architecture, a monumental gate with several passageways separated by rows of columns.

Propylon – In Greek architecture, a gate with a single passageway.

Proskenion – In Greek theatres, a platform in front of a stage building (skene) which played the role of a stage on which actors performed.

Prostyle – A type of rectangular Greek temple fronted by a columned portico.

Prytaneion – In ancient Greece, the headquarters of the Prytaneis, important state officials.

Pulpitum – In Roman theatres, the equivalent of the Greek proskenion.

Pylon – Towers that flanked the entrance to an Egyptian temple.

Relief – A sculpture or ornament projecting from a background.

Rostra (In Latin, rostrum = the prow of a ship) – A podium in a Roman forum. Its name derives from a podium in the Roman Forum of Rome, which was decorated with the prows of warships.

Rython – A vessel in the form of a horn. Its lower section was normally shaped like a human head or an animal.

Scenae Frons – In Roman theatres, the equivalent of the Greek skene, but with a much more elaborate and decorated façade.

Sebasteion – A building or room used in the cult of the deified Roman emperors (Sebastoi in Greek) in the eastern part of the Imperium Romanum, where Greek was the dominant language. The equivalent of the Latin 'augusteum'.

Scarab – An amulet, most often made of steatite or faience, in the shape of a naturally depicted beetle (Scarabaeus Sacer) with a richly decorated base.

Skene – In Greek theatres, a stage building providing the background for the stage on which actors performed (proskenion).

Stele – A stone burial slab, normally covered in relief decoration or inscriptions.

Stoa – In Greek architecture, a columned portico closed off by a rear wall or a row of rooms.

Stomion – In tholos tombs, the passage between the dromos and the funerary chamber.

Stucco – Plaster or calcareous cement render, plain or modelled.

Stylobate – In Greek architecture, the highest of the three levels of the crepidoma on which a temple stood.

Teathron – The viewing area in Greek theatres, most often in the shape of a horseshoe surrounding the orchestra.

Temenos – An enclosed area used in cult worship. A sacred precinct.

Templum in antis (In Latin = Temple between antae) – In ancient architecture, a small, rectangular temple with an entry on its shorter side through a lobby located between antae.

Tepidarium – In Roman baths, a room with a warm pool.

Therme – A complex of public baths in a Roman city used for bathing, social gatherings and during leisure time.

Tetrastyle – A building with four columns in its façade.

Tholos – 1. A tomb consisting of a round funerary chamber to which a corridor (dromos) led, most often entirely covered by a tumulus; 2. In ancient architecture, a circular building.

Torus – A large, semi-circular, convex moulding.

Triclinium – A room with three benches designed for dining, sometimes as part of a funeral.

Triglyph – In the Doric order, an element of the entablature in the shape of a four-sided slab. It has two vertical grooves that divide it into three parts.

Tumulus – A mound of earth, kurgan.

Tympanum – The triangular, interior area of a gable in a temple or other building, often decorated with bas-reliefs.

Vestibule – A type of lobby in Roman houses or buildings of public use.

Xenon – In ancient Greece, a type of hotel where one could stay the night for a fee.

Xoanon – A primitive statue of a god, most often in the form of a plank or wooden post embedded in a vestment, often with a terracotta or stone mask instead of a face.

Xystos – In an ancient gymnasium, a long portico with a covered track used for running practice.

SELECTED BIBLIOGRAPHY

General:

Alcock S. E., *Graecia Capta. The landscapes of Roman Greece*, Cambridge University Press 1996.

Biers W. R., *The Archaeology of Greece*, Cornell University Press 1987.

Dinsmoor W. B., T*he Architecture of Ancient Greece: An Account of its Historic Development*, London 1975.

Iakovidis S. E., *Mycenae-Epidauros. Argos-Tiryns-Nauplion. A complete guide to the museums and archaeological sites of the Argolid*, Athens 1998.

Lawrence A. W., *Greek Architecture*, Yale University Press 1996.

Marinatos N., Hägg R. (eds.), *Greek Sanctuaries. New approaches*, Routledge 1993.

Mee Ch., *Greek Archaeology. A Thematic Approach*, Wiley-Blackwell 2011.

Mee Ch., Spawforth A., *Greece. An Oxford Archaeological Guide*, Oxford University Press 2001.

Olalla P., *Mythological Atlas of Greece*, Athens 2002.

Pedley J., *Sanctuaries and the Sacred in the Ancient Greek World*, Cambridge University Press 2006.

Tomlinson R. A., *Greek Sanctuaries*, London 1976.

Travlos J., *Bildlexikon zur Topographie des antiken Attika*, Tübingen 1988.

Whitley J., *The Archaeology of Ancient Greece*, Cambridge University Press 2001.

Pausanias:

Akujärvi J., *Researcher, Traveller, Narrator. Studies in Pausanias' Periegesis*, Studia Graeca et latina Lundensia 12, Lund 2005.

Alcock S. E., Cherry J. F., Elsner J. (eds.), *Pausanias. Travel and Memory in Roman Greece*, Oxford University Press 2001.

Georgopoulou M., Guilmet C., Pikoulas Y. A., Staikos K. Sp., Tolias G. (eds.), *Following Pausanias. The Quest for Greek Antiquity*, OAK Knoll Press, Kotinos 2007.

Habicht Ch., *Pausanias' Guide to Ancient Greece*, University of California Press, Berkeley, Los Angeles, London 1998.

Hutton W., *Describing Greece. Landscape and Literature in the Periegesis of Pausanias*, Cambridge University Press 2005.

Pausanias, *Pausanias Description of Greece*, translation by W.H.S. Jones and H.A. Ormerod, 4 Volumes, Cambridge, MA, Harvard University Press, London, William Heinemann Ltd. 1918.

Athens:

Brommer F., *Die Akropolis von Athen*, Darmstadt 1985.

Brouskari M., *The Monuments of the Acropolis*, Athens 1997.

Camp J., *The Athenian Agora*, London 1986.

Camp J. M., *The Archaeology of Athens*, Yale University Press 2001.

Hurwit J., *The Athenian Acropolis. History, Mythology, and Archaeology from the Neolithic Era to the Present*, Cambridge University Press 1998.

Knigge U., *The Athenian Kerameikos: History, Monuments, Excavations*, Athens 1991.

Mauzy C. A., Camp II J. McK. (eds.), *The Athenian Agora. New perspectives on an Ancient Site*, Philipp von Zabern 2009.

Neils J., *The Parthenon: From Antiquity to the Present*, Cambridge University Press 2005.

Rhodes R. F., *Architecture and Meaning on the Athenian Acropolis*, Cambridge University Press 1995.

Thompson H. A., *The Athenian Agora: A Guide to the Excavation and Museum*, 2nd ed., Athens 1962.

Thompson H. A., Wycherley R. E., The Agora of Athens. *The History, Shape and Uses o fan Ancient City Center*, The Athenian Agora, Vol. XIV, Princeton, New Jersey 1972.

Tolle-Kastenbein R., *Das Olympeion in Athen*, Köln 1994.

Travlos J., *Pictorial Dictionary of Athens*, London 1971.

Wycherley R. E., *The Stones of Athens*, Princeton 1978.

Sounion:

Abramson H., *A Hero Shrine for Phrontis at Sounion?*, California Studies in Classical Antiquity 12, p. 1–19.

Davaras C., *Sounion. Archaeological guide*, Athens 1979.

Dinsmoor W. B. Jr., *Guide to Sounion*, Athens 1970.

Plommer W. H., *Three Attic Temples, Part II. The Temple of Poseidon*, The Annual of the British School at Athens 45 (1950), p. 78–94.

Plommer W. H., *The Temple of Poseidon on Cape Sunium: Some Further Questions*, The Annual of the British School at Athens 55 (1960), p. 218–233.

Sinn U., *Sunion*, Antike Welt 23 (1992), p. 175–190.

Delphi:

Amandry P. P., Chamoux F., *Guide de Delphes. Le Musée*, Sites et monuments 6, École Française d'Athènes 1991.

Bommelaer J.-Fr., *La construction du temple classique de Delphes*, Bulletin de la Correspondance Hellénique 107 (1983), p. 191–216.

Bommelaer J.-F., *Marmaria, le sanctuaire d'Athéna à Delphes*, Sites et monuments 16, École Française d'Athènes 1997.

Bommelaer J.-F., Laroche D., *Guide de Delphes. Le Site*, Sites et monuments 7, École Française d'Athènes 1991.

Delcourt M., *L' Oracle de Delphes*, Paris 1981.

Hoyle P., *Delphi*, London 1967.

Middleton J. H., *The Temple of Apollo at Delphi*, Journal of Hellenic Studies 9 (1888), p. 282–322.

Partida E. C., *The Treasuries at Delphi. An Architectural Study*, Studies in Mediterranean Archaeology Pocket-Book 160, Paul Åströms Förlag, Jonsered 2000.

Poulsen F., *Delphi*, London 1920.

Roux G., *Delphes, son oracle et ses dieux*, Paris 1976.

Roux G., *La tholos d'Athena Pronaia dans son sanctuaire de Delphes*, Comptes rendus de l'Académie des Inscriptions et Belles-Lettres 1988, p. 290–309.

Corinth:

Bellinger A. R., Blegen C. W., Broneer O., Stillwell R., *Acrocorinth: Excavations in 1926*, Corinth III, Part I Harvard University Press 1930.

Bookidis N., Stroud R. S., *Apollo and the Archaic Temple at Corinth*, Hesperia 73,3 (2004), p. 401–426.

Dunbabin T. J., *The Early History of Corinth*, Journal of Hellenic Studies 68 (1948), p. 59–69.

Fowler H. N., Stillwell R., *Introduction, Topography, Architecture*, Corinth I, Cambridge 1932.

Hill B. H., *The Springs: Peirene, Sacred Spring, Glauke*, Corinth I, Part VI, Princeton 1965.

Hoskins-Walbank M. E., *Pausanias, Octavia and Temple E at Corinth*, The Annual of the British School at Athens 84 (1989), p. 361–394.

Powell B., *The Temple of Apollo at Corinth*, American Journal of Archaeology 9,1 (1905), p. 44–63.

Salmon J. B., *Wealthy Corinth. A History of the City to 338 BC*, Oxford 1984.

Sears Jr. J. M., *The Lechaeum Road and the Propylaea at Corinth*, American Journal of Archaeology 6,4 (1902), p. 439–454.

Stillwell R. et al., *Architecture*, Corinth I, Part II, Cambridge 1941.

Williams II Ch. K., Bookidis N., *Corinth. The Centenary 1896–1996*, Corinth XX, Princeton 2003.

Williams II Ch. K., Zervos O. H., *Corinth, 1990: Southeast Corner of Temenos E*, Hesperia 60,1 (1991), p. 1–58.

Mycenae:

French E. B., *Mycenae. Agamemnon's Capital: the Site and its Setting*, 2002.

Iakovides Sp., *Mycenae in the Light of Recent Discoveries*, in: E. De Miro, L. Godart, A. Sacconi (eds), Atti e Memorie des Secondo Congresso Internazionale di Micenologia (Roma-Napoli, 14–20 ottobre 1991), Roma 1996, p. 1039–1049.

Iakovides Sp., French E., *Archaeological Atlas of Mycenae*, 2003.

Mylonas G., *Ancient Mycenae. The Capital City of Agamemnon*, Princeton 1957.

Mylonas G., *Mycenae and the Mycenaean Age*, Princeton 1966.

Mylonas G., *Mycenae. A Giude to its Ruins and its History*, Athens 1977.

Schliemann H., Gladstone W. E., *Mycenae. A Narrative of Researches and Discoveries at Mycenae and Tiryns*, New York 1880.

Wace A. J. B., *Chamber Tombs at Mycenae*, Oxford 1932.

Wace A. J. B., *Mycenae. An Archaeological History and Guide*, Oxford University Press 1949.

Epidaurus:

Burford A., *The Greek Temple Builders at Epidauros, A social and economic study of building in the Asklepian sanctuary, during the fourth and early third centuries b.c.*, Liverpool University Press 1969.

Büsing H., *Zur Bauplanung der Tholos von Epidauros*, Archäologische Mitteilungen 102 (1987), p. 225–258

Elderkin G. W., *Tholos and Abaton at Epidaurus*, American Journal of Archaeology 15,2 (1911), p. 161–167.

von Gerkan A., Miller-Wiener W., *Das Theater Von Epidauros*, Stuttgart 1961.

Käppel L., *Das Theater von Epidauros*, Jahrbuch des Deutschen Archäologischen Instituts 104 (1989), p. 83–106

Roux G., *L'Architecture de l' Argolide aux IV et III siècles*, Paris 1961.

Tomlinson R. A., *Epidauros*, London 1983.

Yalouris N., *Die Skulpturen des Asklepiostempels in Epidauros*, Antike Plastik 21, Munich 1992.

Sparta and Menelaion:

Cartledge P. A., *Sparta and Lakonia. A regional history 1300–362 BC*, London 1979.

Cartledge P. A., Spawforth A.J.S., *Hellenistic and Roman Sparta: a Tale of Two Cities*, London 1989.

Catling H. W., *Sparta, Menelaion I: The Bronze Age*, The Annual of the British School at Athens Supplementary Volume No. 45, Athens 2009.

Cavanagh W. G., Walker S. E. C. (eds), *Sparta in Lnconia. Proceedings of the 19th British Museum Classical Colloquium held with the British School at Athens and King's and University Colleges, London 6–8 December 1995*, British School at Athens Studies 4. London 1998.

Kourinou-Pikoula E., *The Monuments of Ancient Sparta*, in: Kaltsas N. (ed.), Athens-Sparta. Catalogue of the exhibition "Athens-Starta" held at the Onasis Cultural Center, New York, December 6, 2006 – May 12, 2007, p. 29–35.

Waywell G. B., Wilkes J. J., *Excavations at Sparta: The Roman Stoa, 1988–91 Part 2*, The Annual of the British School at Athens 89 (1994), p. 377–432.

Waywell G. B., Wilkes J. J., *Excavations at the Ancient Theatre of Sparta 1995–1998: Preliminary Report*, The Annual of the British School at Athens 94 (1999), p. 437–455.

Waywell G., *Sparta and its Topography*, Bulletin of the Institute of Classical Studies 43, 2010, p. 1–26.

Olympia:

Ashmole B., Yalouris N., *Olympia, The Sculptures of the Temple of Zeus*, London 1967.

Barringer J. M., *The Temple of Zeus at Olympia, Heroes, and Athletes*, Hesperia 74,2 (2005), p. 211–241.

Berichte über die Ausgrabungen in Olympia, Bd. 1–12, Berlin 1937–2003.

Die Ausgrabungen zu Olympia, Bd. 1–5, Berlin 1876–1881.

Dörpfeld W., *Alt-Olympia. Untersuchungen und Ausgrabungen zur Geshichte des ältesten Heiligtums von Olympia und der älteren griechischen Kunst*, Bd. 1–2, Berlin 1935.

Drees L., *Olympia. Gods, Artists and Athletes*, London 1968.

Herrmann H.-V., *Olympia. Heiligtum und Wettkampfstätte*, Hirmer Verlag 1972.

Kaltsas N., *Olympia*, Athens 2004.

Kyrieleis H. (Hrsg.), *Olympia 1875-2000. 125 Jahre deutsche Ausgrabungen. Internationales Symposion, Berlin 9.-11. November 2000*, Philipp von Zabern 2002.

Kyrieleis H., *Olympia. Archäologie eines Heiligtums*, Philipp von Zabern 2011.

Mallwitz A., *Olympia und seine Bauten*, Munich 1972.

Mallwitz A., Herrmann H.-V. (Hrsg.), *Die Funde aus Olympia. Ergebnisse 100-jähriger Ausgrabungstätigkeit*, Athen 1980.

Olympia. Die Ergebnisse der vom Deutschen Reich veranstalteten Ausgrabung, Bd. I–V, Berlin 1890–1897.

Olympische Forschungen, Bd. 1–33, Berlin 1944–2011.

www.ingramcontent.com/pod-product-compliance
Lightning Source LLC
Chambersburg PA
CBHW072001040426
42447CB00009B/1430

* 9 7 8 8 3 9 3 5 7 5 7 1 8 *